*The Grace
of Great Things*

The Grace
of Great Things

CREATIVITY
AND INNOVATION

Robert Grudin

TICKNOR & FIELDS · NEW YORK

For information about permission to reproduce selections
from this book, write to Permissions, Ticknor & Fields,
Houghton Mifflin Company, 2 Park Street,
Boston, Massachusetts 02108.

Library of Congress Cataloging-in-Publication Data

Grudin, Robert.
The grace of great things : creativity and innovation /
Robert Grudin.
p.   cm.
Includes bibliographical references.
ISBN 0-89919-940-2
ISBN 0-395-58868-5 (pbk.)
1. Creative ability.   2. Creative ability — Social aspects.
I. Title.
BF408.G72   1990   89-77195
153.3'5 — dc20   CIP

Printed in the United States of America

HAD 10 9 8 7 6 5 4 3 2 1

Four chapters, or parts of chapters, have appeared, in different
form, in the following publications: Chapter 2, Inspiration, in *The
Phenomenon of Change,* ed. Lisa Taylor (New York: Cooper-Hewitt
Museum, 1984); Chapter 3, Discovery, *Northwest Review,* Spring
1986; Chapter 15, Higher Education and Classical Wholeness,
Claremont Review of Books, Fall 1983. Part of Chapter 10,
Courage, appeared in *Old Oregon,* Summer 1989.

The author gratefully acknowledges permission to quote from the
following poems: Robert Frost, "Mowing." From *The Poetry of
Robert Frost* by Edward Connery Lathem. Copyright 1934, 1969,
by Holt, Rinehart and Winston. Copyright 1962 by Robert Frost.
Reprinted by arrangement with Henry Holt and Company, Inc.
Wallace Stevens, "The Woman in Sunshine." Copyright 1950 by
Wallace Stevens. Reprinted from *The Collected Poems of Wallace
Stevens,* by permission of Alfred A. Knopf, Inc.

To Peter, David, and Wendy

Acknowledgments

I am grateful to two scholars whose influence is most apparent in Chapter 4, Analysis. Conversations with Svi Lanir during the spring and summer of 1986 inspired the section Mystery that concludes the chapter. Jacques Barzun thoroughly edited an early version of the chapter, offering criticism so pertinent that it provoked a complete reworking of the book. Richard Todd of Ticknor & Fields was instrumental in the final revision, and my wife, Michaela Paasche Grudin, gave insightful counsel all the way through. The Humanities Center of the University of Oregon provided support for travel to libraries. I am grateful, finally, to my students in the Honors College of the University of Oregon in 1984–1985 for encouragement, advice, and the polite harassment that advanced my study in this field.

Contents

Preface

Creativity and innovation are concepts so dear to modern culture that their very mention excites immediate approval. These ideas lie near the heart of our humanity. We see human civilization as having risen to eminence among the other species through political, scientific, and technological innovation. We prize a cultural heritage that is rich in artistic creativity. We credit liberal democracy, itself an eighteenth-century innovation, with providing the matrix in which creative enterprise has taken shape. We value creativity because we are aware that civilization has, in large measure, created itself.

Yet we have shown comparatively little curiosity about the birth and growth of innovation — the ways in which creative impulse develops into pathfinding achievement. Granted, psychological studies of creativity abound. But such studies generally ignore the ethical and social contexts of creativity and fail to treat the issues that spring up as the result of innovative action. Perhaps we are careless about creativity and innovation precisely because, up to now, we have had so much of them. Critics who maintain that we take our freedoms for granted should place special emphasis on that most precious freedom of all, the liberty implicit in the creation of new ideas and new forms.

The preservation of this freedom is especially important. As I write at the start of the 1990s, the West faces growing outside competition in technological progress and economic power. Analysts have pointed to fatigue on several fronts: outworn tools, rigid organizational structures, impaired communications, vacuous education, moral weakness. We have ample evidence of new ideas rejected as threats to "security," of long-term planning dismissed in favor of ready gain. Interest groups clash with one another over the control of existing freedoms rather than using those which they have productively or cooperating to create new ones.

To treat these problems, we must first locate their causes. We must distinguish between those causes which are specific to our times and those which are universal in history.

This book attempts such a study.

It could just as well be the words that a certain monk is said to have repeated to young Michel Colombe almost five hundred years ago, these words: *Travaille, petit, regarde tout ton saoul et le clocher à jour de Saint-Pol, et les belles oeuvres des compaignons, regarde, aime le bon Dieu, et tu auras la grace des grandes choses.* — And thou shalt have the grace of great things. Perhaps an inner feeling had so spoken, endlessly more quiet than the monk's voice, to the youth [Rodin] at one of his crossroads in his early days. For it was precisely this he sought: the grace of great things.

— Rainer Maria Rilke, *Rodin*

PART I

The Creative Mind

1 Introduction

STUDIES OF CREATIVITY usually recount the actions of genius. One such study begins with Archimedes' discovery of the principles of displacement and specific gravity, another with the triumphs of Copernicus, Kepler, and Einstein. These are classic examples of creativity at work, and the descriptions are excellent. But missing in all three cases is intuition about the reader sitting with book in hand, the poor reader who looks up and glances away in frustration, thinking, "I am not Einstein, nor was meant to be."

This complaint makes perfect sense. The monumental achievement of great minds has little to do with the problems that dog us in personal life. We are less interested in achievement itself than in the slow steps by which it can be approached. Show us Einstein growing up, so we can appreciate the youthful wonder that he stole from time and kept into old age. Show us Archimedes on a bad day, when he achieved nothing but a few angry doodles in the sand, so we can understand the enormous importance of mood and mental tone to anyone with a creative project in hand. Show us how genius deals with its own mistakes and how normal, hardworking people can be surprised by bursts of creativity. Specify for us, in terms that touch our own experience, the exuberance and patience, the courage and humility, that enable creative people to break out through the boundaries of the past with each new thought.

Most of all, perhaps, we wish to capture an experience that seems common to creative achievement of all sorts: the moment of sudden insight. We would hold this moment in stop action until we have sketched its shape and preserved its essence. But even when we have experienced them ourselves, these vivid moments evaporate like dreams. Did lines of thought develop slowly or happen suddenly? Did one thought precede another, or did both occur at once? The past self-destructs in creating the present. Our discoveries so reshape reality that we cannot remember what we were like before we had them.

Yesterday I sat at my desk and could not write. I fidgeted, typed a few aimless words onto the computer screen, and stared at them until they began to shimmer. My back ached.

I glanced at the clock and noticed that two hours had passed, as though in two minutes, except I suddenly felt old and very tired. I walked out of the office and looked for someone to chat with.

When I got back, things were no better. The office looked stricken and skewed, like architecture photographed at the moment of collapse. The blank computer screen seemed like a mirror of my mind, and when I appealed to my memory for a new rush of confidence, my memory replied, with the impact of a sudden and unimpeachable revelation, that nothing I had ever done had been of much account.

To top it off, I noticed for the first time that every horizontal surface in the office — computer, clock, fan, radio, typewriter, telephone — was encrusted with blackening grime, and that this grime was defacing my office as obscenely as my own inactivity was defacing my brain. I got up again, found a bottle of Windex, and worked like a demon, rubbing away about a pint of dissolving filth.

When I was through cleaning I sat down and at once started writing freely.

What does all this suggest about creativity? To me it suggests that the moment of insight is impossible to formulate or prescribe because of the immense importance of nonverbal, noncerebral factors in the process we call thinking. In my case you could see these factors working in five ways:

1. My task — a pretty simple job when viewed *abstractly* — became instead an *emotional* challenge to my control of ideas and my sense of dignity as a writer.
2. This challenge, irrationally exaggerated, produced physiological symptoms that fed back negatively into my conscious awareness. In other words, doubting made me feel bad, and feeling bad made me doubt the more.
3. The syndrome of doubts and pains was augmented by an ethical dimension in which I compared myself negatively with other members of society.
4. The impulse to clean my office stemmed from a visual, rather than verbal, metaphor connecting my self-doubts with the dirt in the room.
5. The task of cleaning extended the metaphor, again nonverbally, to produce a catharsis that eased and dissolved my mental paralysis.

My office-cleaning experience underlines some of the central premises of this book: The generation of ideas involves factors that are not exclusively cerebral, factors that include the physiology, the emotions, and the outer world. We do not create, or even learn, by conscious concentration alone. The mind is not an instrument distinct from the "body" it inhabits and from that body's surrounding environment. It communicates freely and profoundly with the noncerebral anatomy, via both the nervous system and the cardiovascular system. It can receive powerful stimuli from outside events, both great and small. Its various structures of language make it an organic part of culture, of history. The mind feeds on all these sources, yet transcends them in its ability to modulate and focus their input. Original thought is the product not of the brain, but of the full self. And "self," as I understand it, is not confined by our skins but defined by our humanity.

This thesis calls into question much of the customary language of ideation and the assumptions on which this language is based. In the first place, "mind" (as I have defined it) is not co-equal with an individual's private or legal identity. The fact that creative productions are always structured in terms of cultural signs (mathematical, visual, linguistic, and so forth) is proof enough of the essentially *social* nature of creativity. Creative achievement, moreover, is characteristically an "offering" to society rather than a solitary amusement; this in turn suggests an individual-society interaction in which society's past or predicted reception of creative achievement becomes one of the directing factors in a creator's work. Thus the modern Western emphasis on individuality, personality, and competition in the creative process dangerously simplifies what this process is all about.

In the second place, modern idioms unfairly compartmentalize the process of thought. To say that we "had an idea" or "solved a problem" or "worked something out" is to imply that mind as discrete "subject" handles idea as discrete "object." Such idioms suggest a mechanical relation between mind and idea, one in which too much emphasis is put on conscious effort and too little on openness and receptivity. Accepting this model, we visualize creativity in terms of dominance and control, as though thinking were a kind of warfare or business.

Such a view is both inaccurate and inhibiting. We no more "have" ideas than ideas "have" us, and indeed the creative process might be simplified if we stopped searching for ideas and simply made room for them to visit. If anything controls or dominates at the moment of inspiration, it is not the mind but the idea, or rather, the suddenly articulated power of our own inner energies. New ideas capture and possess the mind that births them; they colonize it and renew its laws. The expansion of any idea is thus also an expansion of self.

For this reason, if for no other, creativity is a classic example of human freedom. We commonly think of freedom as the ability to define alternatives and choose between them. The creative mind exceeds this liberty in being able to redefine itself and reality at large, generating whole new sets of alternatives. Intellectual history is punctuated by such redefinitions, by creative acts that open new reaches of expression and inquiry. In this sense we can call creative vision the edge of freedom, the evolutionary faculty by which, down through history, we have redefined our world and ourselves.

Because it is a radical act of freedom, creative achievement is a heroic process that requires, in all its permutations, specific strengths of character. This is not to say that creative people are necessarily "good" or even "happy" people in societal terms; I mean that certain heroic habits of mind seem to inform their attitude toward their own work. It is impossible to speak of these strengths without using moral language: words like "integrity," "courage," "endurance," and "freedom" itself. These virtues, irrelevant to the more routine uses of intelligence, become essential when one's challenges involve self-discovery, spirited inquiry, and individual expression. They are necessary because of the extreme difficulty of original thinking, which must be developed over long periods of time, quite often without adequate societal support. Since creativity partakes of such heroic virtues, we must see it as having a moral dimension.

If all these topics seem interesting, one may well ask why there has not been a flood of books about them. Much important work has been done on the *cognitive* aspects of creativity. But what of the moral and social dimensions? Why, in a society that professes to admire all valid forms of novelty, have we not seen more major work on the full profile of innovative thought?

The answer, as I have suggested, would seem to lie in widely held modern Western assumptions about creativity and freedom. As beneficiaries of a great liberal tradition, we assume ourselves to be fully open to innovative ideas. As graduates of advanced universities, we assume ourselves to be conversant with the basic principles of invention and interpretation. Our specific assumptions about these subjects surface in the way we use key words — "analysis," "reason," "objective," "teaching," "integrity," and even "creativity" and "freedom." These words may serve us well enough in casual conversation, but when used in serious investigations they pose a special problem, namely that, as concepts deemed self-evident, they put a damper on inquiry itself. Why bother inquiring into what we already know?

But precisely this sort of self-inquiry must be undertaken by any book that deals fairly with creative and innovative thought. No society, however sophisticated or liberal, is wholly free of superstition, and superstition is most likely to lurk unnoticed in assumptions that have rooted in language. Unwarranted assumptions about the nature of thought are particularly subtle and debilitating, and of these, perhaps most dangerous is the assumption that our thought is free.

Real freedom, however, makes no assumptions. It invariably questions all the assumptions it finds and in so doing takes up the absurd but inevitable task of testing and defining itself. Inquiry into the nature of creativity must therefore address not only its sources and principles but the societal quirks and foibles that restrain it.

We cannot sketch the full profile of creativity without consideration of these negative traits. We read with indignation of their past effects: the legalized assassination of Socrates and Christ, the church resistance to reform and inquiry during the Renaissance, the disdain or neglect, by their contemporaries, of artists like Bach and van Gogh. We speak with disapproval of totalitarian regimes whose rigid fabric proscribes most forms of creative expression. Can it be that the injustice that applied in other ages and cultures has failed to affect us alone? This book will chart the extent to which intolerance, neglect, and repression may operate in "liberal" society: how our resistance to our own creativity may be projected out against our peers, how our very language and institutions may discourage innovation.

For these reasons, and others as well, the study of creativity holds both pleasure and pain. Of all the kinds of joy, none perhaps is so pure as that occasioned by sudden insight. To come to terms independently with a new idea is to celebrate, in the broadest sense of the word, the reality of nature and to appreciate fully one's own human presence. But creativity does not confine itself to happy subjects, or always bring happy results. Too many examples of tragic vision, or of genius in the service of malice, argue the contrary. Moreover, though creative insight may be delightful in itself, it normally is predicated on training, prolonged concentration, and exhausting practice that are not pleasant in the same sense.

Finally, creativity is dangerous. We cannot open ourselves to new insight without endangering the security of our prior assumptions. We cannot propose new ideas without risking disapproval and rejection. Creative achievement is the boldest initiative of mind, an adventure that takes its hero simultaneously to the rim of knowledge and the limits of propriety. Its pleasure is not the comfort of the safe harbor, but the thrill of the reaching sail.

The study that follows is an effort to locate the sources of creative energy and to chart the paths and pitfalls that lie between creative energy and effective innovation. To this end, I have divided it into three sections, the first, The Creative Mind, dealing with the origins of creative expression, the second, The Ethics of Creativity, examining the relationship between creativity and moral values, and the third, The Politics of Innovation, discussing a variety of ways in which social forces — educational, historical, and ideological — can feed back into the creative process.

2 *Inspiration*

The strokes of genius are but the outcome of a continuous habit of inquiry that grasps clearly and distinctly all that is involved in the simple things that anyone can understand.

— Bernard J. F. Lonergan, *Insight*

The idea seems absurd, but I can find no flaw in it.

— Johannes Kepler

THE WORD "inspiration" originally meant a breath of divinity or transfusion of soul received from the gods by some deserving individual. The word now denotes the experience of a sudden insight that cuts across categories or otherwise leaps over the normal steps of reasoning. Though both these definitions are helpful, it is the ancient one, with its religious overtones, that seems to hold more psychological truth. To be inspired is to surrender one's mind to a new force, heedless and powerful. Experiencing inspiration is like leaving the world of effort and abandoning oneself to an irresistible flow, like a canoeist drawn into the main channel of a rapids, or a bodysurfer who catches a fine wave just below the crest.

Yet these metaphors do not describe the full experience. If in-

spiration partakes of abandonment or surrender, it also, and simultaneously, partakes of assertion and authority. It is as
though we know as our own the power that has overcome us, as
though the act of surrender holds the mystery of dominion.
Our aquatic metaphors will work only if we imagine the canoeist becoming one with the river, the surfer one with the
wave: if we see each as participating for a few moments in a
vastly larger and more powerful identity.

Why is inspiration given to some people and withheld from
others? The key word in our ancient definition is "deserving."
All inspired individuals are, in some way, prepared for the experience. A corporation lawyer, unstudied in math beyond simple arithmetic, cannot expect sudden revelations about non-
Euclidian geometry; a football player, dreamily jetting home
from a road game, is unlikely to be visited by new insights
into the gasification of oil. If inspiration is indeed an abandonment and a transcendence, it is nonetheless impossible without
groaning effort, without the painful winning of skill. Here,
as before, inspiration suggests the combination of an active
principle — hard-earned expertise — with a passive principle —
unencumbered and trustful receptivity.

Many writers have sought to analyze the process of inspiration, and one very illuminating example of such analysis (from
Rollo May's *The Courage to Create*) is included in the notes to
this chapter. But inspiration, like freedom and innovation, is an
idea that cannot be specified without being diminished. Too
many variables implicit in the process — genetic inheritance,
mood, circumstance, and so forth — make the analysis of inspiration a fragmentary procedure at best. For similar reasons, specific inspirations obviously cannot be purposed or designed. To
labor for inspiration, wait for it, reason toward it, or in any way
address it as a thing in itself is, in effect, to lose one's openness
to it. But even if we cannot specify or command inspiration, we
can, I think, practice deserving it. The lives of people who are

inspired or inventive possess a number of characteristics in common. Many of these characteristics are less inborn virtues (though seen together they look like "talent" or "genius") than plain habits, difficult to cultivate perhaps, but nonetheless far from superhuman. Collectively, these habits might be called an ethos of inspiration — not a birthright but a demanding and integral code.

Let me try to summarize.

PASSION FOR WORK

By this I do not mean the passionate longing for some as-yet-unwon goal, but rather the delight of being totally within one's own element — of identifying fully with one's work and seeing it as an expression of one's own character. Such passion, which is generally more characteristic of artists and the self-employed than it is of salaried workers, can nonetheless be cultivated in any work that carries a high degree of personal responsibility.

This affection must be so strong and genuine that it persists during leisure hours and even makes its way into dreams. At leisure or at rest the mind knows no deadlines or constraints and is open to its inner energies. It can perceive wholly new aspects of a subject or see the whole subject in new ways. Leisure and rest not only relieve the mind from work but also allow it to appreciate work more fully.

But in one sense the passion transcends the work/leisure distinction altogether. Society generally regards leisure as being the opposite of work: the antidote for work's debilitating effects. In the creative life, however, no such opposition exists. Creative work is self-expression, self-fulfillment. As such it is a pleasure that ranks with sport and love and laughter and all the other better things of life. In the creative life, leisure is not a contrary of work but rather a complement to it. Thus elements from work can extend into leisure hours, while work hours, conversely, partake of the freedom and delight normally associated with leisure.

FIDELITY

Inspiration tends to visit people who renew contact with the major challenges of some ongoing project every day and who set no time limit on their involvement. Such people can accept the failure of a day's effort or a week's enterprise, confident at once that the past has brought better results and that the future will offer new opportunities. Their confidence in turn gives them that calm attention which is open to new ideas. They belong to their work, and it rewards their commitment with unexpected discovery.

Fidelity also operates, over shorter periods of time, in the act of prolonged concentration. Attention to one's subject should be so generous, extended, and intimate that the idea virtually inhabits the mind. It might be objected that concentration on a single subject blinds us to the ramifications and analogies that characterize inventive thought. But here, I think, the opposite is true. For each subject, expanded by concentration until it occupies the full volume of the mind, becomes a kind of world in itself, crowded with the forms and potentialities that tie it to the rest of experience.

LOVE OF THE PROBLEMATIC

Distaste for work and consequent deadness to inspiration often can be traced to a hatred of problems, ingrained since early childhood and probably the result of an educational system that emphasizes "solutions" rather than process. It can be argued, on the other hand, that the mind instinctively *loves* problems, not only because it likes to draw its own conclusions but also for the sheer fun of venturing into something new. To be open to inspiration, one must cultivate a leaning for the problematic, a chronic attraction to things that do not totally fit, agree, or make sense. Inspired ideas are less often solutions to old problems than newly discovered or totally reformulated problems — problems "created" like brilliant works of art.

Many creative people initially are seen as troublemakers, simply because their vigorous and uncompromising analysis exposes problems that previously had been ignored. At their best, such people, like Copernicus, Darwin, and Freud, turn out to be the founders of new forms of order; the greatest advocates of order — Plato, Aquinas, Newton, and others — have also been notable for their love of problems. Indeed, the true lover of problems must be a lover of order, and vice versa.

LOVE OF BEAUTY

Our sense of beauty is generally restricted to those categories (art, music, love, nature) to which aesthetic language is applied by our culture. But independent insight in all fields involves in some way the experience of beauty. In fact, the thrill conveyed by inspiration in any field is perhaps best described as coming from a sense of *participation* in beauty, a momentary unity between a perceived beauty of experience and a perceiving beauty of mind.

A healthy sense of beauty is one of the key factors in the passion for work that dissolves the work/leisure dichotomy. To see beauty in professional experience is to build an important connection between our "public" and "private" selves, between the rational tasks that we perform and our latent psychic energies. Readers may object that their own professional lives

— repetitive, cluttered, and generally demoralizing — allow no opportunity for the perception of beauty. In extreme cases, this is true. Nonetheless, as I hope to show, no job that requires independent problem solving or leadership or effective speaking or writing need be devoid of beauty.

A SENSE OF WHOLENESS

To honor wholeness is to understand that every distinct object or phenomenon — a living cell, a musical tone, a thought, a kiss — is, on the one hand, a special combination of interacting elements, and that it is, on the other hand, itself an element interacting in larger forms. To think holistically is to presume the continuity of experience: to appreciate wholeness in the areas one knows well and to seek it in other areas.

Holistic thinkers are more open to inspiration than others because they instinctively ask questions that others do not: What inner components give this thing its form? Of what larger forms is this thing an element? How does its participation in these larger forms affect its identity? These questions open up a variety of perspectives, make the mind fertile for new ideas, and equip us to appreciate the apparent discontinuities — the surprising anomalies — that can result in important discoveries.

BOLDNESS

We think of innovators as being bold, even arrogant. But external boldness would be useless without its inner counterpart, a courage toward ideas. To think creatively is to walk at the edge of chaos. In thinking the original, we risk thinking the ridiculous. In opening the way for a few good ideas, we open the way for many bad ones: lopsided equations, false syllogisms, and pure nonsense dished up by unhindered impulse. Even valid ideas, at the moment of discovery, give one a sense of giddiness, a fleeting impression of being drunk and sixteen. To be attentive to new messages, to sift them for validity and mercilessly reject the invalid, and to follow good ideas in spite of their forbidding strangeness all take a kind of courage. And this courage, once internalized, is often projected into the innovator's relations with the world at large.

Imagine that the creative mind is a lively child who is taught a number of rules by strict guardians. These rules include —

- Always be helpful.
- Always make sense.
- Consult the authorities.
- Exceptions prove the rule.
- Never disturb your neighbors' calm.
- Avoid anything that makes you laugh or cry.
- If any of the above upsets you, consult an adviser.

— and other such courtesies. The child sees the value of these rules but cannot reconcile them with reality. The child knows that breaking the rules is dangerous, but obeying them is psychologically intolerable. In breaking the rules, the child learns courage.

CONSEQUENCE

Consequence, as I define it here, is the habit of seeing every major juncture in a given study as part of a process rather than a thing in itself. To be "consequent" is to view every success as a step in an ongoing venture, every failure as a substantial discovery in a mission of trial and error. To be consequent is to be at once persistent and discerning. So armed, one is less vulnerable to distraction, procrastination, and other symptoms of despair.

The importance of this habit lies in its opening up and freeing time for the creative process. For consequent people, time ceases to be differentiated into separate compartments like beginning or end, success or failure, and becomes instead a continuum whose stretch holds no big terrors or surprises. Lack of temporal constraint allows room for the concentration and involvement that can lead to inspiration. A sense of consequence can prevent us from rushing jobs; it can provide us with patience during the long, slow work that lies at the beginning of almost every large project.

INNOCENCE AND PLAYFULNESS

No matter how much they already know or think they know, inventive people have a way of wiping the slate clean when they consider a new project. Preconceptions can militate against valid insight; investigators who insist on building exclusively upon past findings equip themselves for defeat. But inventive people seem able at once to use the past well and to project their new impressions on a blank screen. Unbiased by tradition or the phantom of certainty, they look into their subject for elemental interrelations: balance/imbalance, harmony/disharmony, form/substance, analogy/distinction, cause/purpose, and others.

I describe all this as "innocence" because it reminds me of babies who sit and play with some household object — a bottle or a bookend. As they feel it, taste it, turn it over and around, the object is something without known purpose or use, without up or down. The object exists as a discrete phenomenon whose internal principles and external relationships, in the crucible of independent study and experiment, are open to redefinition. This uncompromising freedom of mind can enliven the whole gamut of innovation, from the wit of a cook who turns a failed mousse into a successful chocolate topping to the genius of Paracelsus, who transformed alchemical principles into the new science of chemistry.

As innocence is without preconception, so also is it without embarrassment. Only such a mind is open to inspiration which typically involves the acceptance of outrageous improbability as simple truth. We might call radical purity of mind naive or even promiscuous in its random availability to notions, but even this metaphor is inadequate. Such a mind is not merely receptive to new data, but ready to redefine *itself* with relation to that data. Such a mind is hungry for the experience that reveals not only the seen but the seer.

COURTESY

History assures us that some great innovators have been highly competitive individuals, self-centered, quick to anger, grasping for honors, jealous of others' success. But it would be inaccurate to conclude that these stormy propensities are basic elements of creativity, and it would be a gross error to presume that ill feeling, even if it is harbored toward competitors, is innate in innovators' attitude toward their own work. Whether or not they are polite to their associates, great innovators address their own studies with appreciation, deference, and even humility; they excel in activities, like the revision or destruction of their own inferior work, that suggest the willing suppression of ego.

An analogous form of civility seems to operate in innovators' attitude toward detail. With the courtesy of a host who gives equal welcome to princes and beggars, the creative mind gives respect and patience to the smallest detail. Such a mind is reluctant to subordinate detail to principle, recognizing that detail is the basis of principle, and that even tiny anomalies in detail can inspire revisions in general laws. The imperious generalizations in which creative people revel would be, psychologically and methodologically, impossible without patient regard for detail.

SUFFERING

Inspiration is related to suffering, but not in the way most people think. The Romantics saw the creative individual as a kind of Faust or an aesthetic Flying Dutchman, doomed by talent to torment and alienation. A more modern version of this myth, common among recent generations, is that inspiration lies somewhere between intoxication and psychosis, that it can result only from some physiological or psychological distortion of one's humanity. While these theories have some value in consoling the uninspired, they do not hold up in history. Creative individuals, even those whom society misprizes, do not necessarily face mental disorders or other woes.

They more generally *do*, however, face temporary but severe pains inherent in the nature of their work. Their pains are symptomatic of many typical phases in the creative process: the failure of experiments, the refutation of hypotheses, the shock of criticism, the endurance of contradictions or anomalies, the reorganization or trashing of one's own material, and the mere awareness that such experiences necessarily await one. In action, these agonies may seem to act as dampers against the creative process, but their extended function is often quite the reverse. Duly faced and endured, like some heavy physical exercise, they can provide the spiritual softening and sensitizing, the exhaustion and humility, that make us amenable to inspiration.

·

REMEMBRANCE

Inspiration is profoundly linked to memory. If innovators are bold and innocent, open and courteous, to present phenomena, they are equally so toward things of the past. They recognize that memory, like everything else about us, is alive and evolving. If nourished and attended, memory of itself offers up new ideas; if nagged and compelled, it belabors us with disconnected axioms, unexamined preconceptions, and other junk parts.

An especially important aspect of memory is our attitude toward the thought of our predecessors. It is striking how many noted revolutionaries and innovators insist that they are maintaining continuity with the past or restoring old ideas that have been corrupted or forgotten. Socrates and Plato look back to Pythagoras and Parmenides, Machiavelli to the Roman Republic, Galileo to Plato and Archimedes, Rousseau to primitive humanity. A central idea in the history of religious innovation is the quest to regain continuity with ancient forms of piety.

One reason for these returns to earlier thought is simple enough. Many new ideas are analogies to, or new applications of, old ones. But another force seems at work as well. To the inspired as well as to their audiences, innovative insights contain a sense of the familiar, the permanent. Inspiration may be the revelation of something completely new, but it is also the rediscovery of something always true.

A SENSE OF THE CONTINUITY
OF PERCEPTION

Inspiration often expresses itself as a sudden connection or closed circuit between ideas that had never before been so connected. The mind is open to inspiration to the extent that it is open to such continuities, whether between details (as with the combination of words in a fresh poetic metaphor) or between larger subject areas (as with some new combination of materials in a manufacturing process). By extension, the sense of continuity can extend to dynamic relationships between whole disciplines or ways of thinking. In *The Act of Creation,* Arthur Koestler names this process bisociation — the dynamic interaction between two normally distinct frames of reference. According to Koestler, all creative thought, from humor to philosophy and science, is bisociational, and creativity derives from a feeling for the implicit continuity of ideas.

But ideas per se are not the only subjects of creative continuity. As I tried to show earlier, in describing office dirt as a metaphor for my mental confusion, noncerebral factors can establish valuable continuities of their own. Such factors include physiological events inside us and just about everything else available to perception. A long jog, with its strong rhythm and sense of physiological expressiveness, is a cathartic metaphor for my own thoughts, especially when I am chatting with another jogger. Contrapuntal music works on me similarly, and sometimes a glance out of my office window, to the graceful Douglas firs that stand to the south, is enough to clear my head.

A SENSE OF OPENNESS

Barraged by information and opinion from all sides, we tend to see the world of inquiry as enclosed space, filled almost to bursting with other people's good ideas and at best affording only small crannies for our personal contributions. To be inventive, on the other hand, is to see the world of inquiry more as an unfinished house of light and shadow, with unglassed windows opening up on indefinite vistas, with doorways and staircases opening to empty space. And rather than threatening, the incompleteness and emptiness seem to beckon. Inventive people live with an absurd but indispensable trust that the next idea that comes to them may be totally new.

The sense of openness is useful, of course, in evaluating the imperatives or limits accepted by a given culture or profession during a given period. Faced with such imperatives or limits, which can range from a theological doctrine to the proper use of paper clips, the open mind simply asks, Does this have to be true? and if not, What theory better fits the facts as I perceive them?

But openness has even greater value in keeping us from being deceived by the *false freedoms* — or rather, the sets of false alternatives — that lurk in culture and language. When Hamlet, for example, becomes convinced that he must either assassinate Claudius or go through life a coward, he entraps himself in a set of socially communicated alternatives that do not suggest the actual extent of human freedom. Inventive people can transcend such alternatives, and their sometimes very serious consequences, by rethinking the problem, and their own relationship to it, from scratch. In redefining problems, they can generate new alternatives.

LIBERTY

More generally, most of us go through life assuming that the world, give or take a tree here or a building there, was meant to be more or less what it is. We tend to accept the status quo, in general terms, as the limit of possibility. The essence of inventiveness lies in trashing this assumption. Creative people intuitively distinguish between cause and purpose, raw material and possible use. They seem to see the world not as static posture but as mobile energy, capable of innumerable configurations. They understand not only that things can change but that they must. Cognate with this understanding is the ability to distinguish between the provincial bylaws of this or that science or social order and the universally applicable canons of nature. In these latter laws they find no prohibitions, only positive directives so grand and persistent that they seem to fill the universe and leave no room for negatives.

On its own scale, the creative mind mirrors and embodies these affirmations. Its positive avowals are so dynamic, so fitting, as to fill its own world. The creative mind chooses justice, moderation, and simplicity, not because their opposites are evil, but because these virtues are the closest possible parallels to the motive freedom of nature.

Looked at together, these habits and attitudes map out the mental "environment" most congenial to inspiration. We might call this habitat a garden of mind, whose order and beauty make it quite different from the staid settings of our day-to-day awareness. A garden is a deliberately ordered system that paradoxically brings its inhabitant closer to nature. Similarly, this garden of mind, whose features are all akin to ethical norms, can be said to open us, via inspiration, to our own inner powers.

For most people, visits to this garden are rare, occurring by surprise and as though by chance. Such visits bring with them a strangeness akin to the sense of being on distant ground. Surprised, even frightened by our own sudden insights, we neglect inquiring into their relation with more permanent aspects of our character. The topics raised above, all relating inspiration to specific personal habits and frames of mind, suggest that such inquiry might have valuable results, that the garden may be less distant than we think.

3 Discovery

It is a fatal fault to reason whilst observing, though so necessary beforehand and so useful afterwards.

— Charles Darwin

WHILE THE WORD "inspiration" suggests a flood of new awareness from within, the word "discovery" suggests the achievement of new awareness as the result of contact with the outside world. At one end of the spectrum of discovery are chance encounters with circumstantial information. At the other are philosophical achievements of the highest order.

Circumstantial discovery occurs when an individual becomes aware of an existing circumstance that may be good or bad and that may or may not be important. Jill discovers that she has the mumps. The garbage man discovers the butler's body under the front stairs. A teacher discovers a single glove lying on a classroom desk. Trotting home to its master's whistle, a dog discovers a bone. Circumstantial discovery is largely a passive phenomenon. Like ships running into icebergs, oil slicks, or pieces of flotsam, we collide with bits of information that happen to be in our way. We do not have to be perceptive to make circumstantial discoveries. We do not even have to be human.

Philosophical discovery — and the word "philosophical" here

means "loving knowledge" in general — partakes of will and has an active dimension. The object of philosophical discovery is information that all of us might be expected to wish to know, information that has general importance and permanent worth. Philosophical discovery may feed on circumstance, but its true object is the law that lies beneath.

THE PSYCHOLOGY OF DISCOVERY

By definition there is something unreasonable about discovery, for discovery suggests surprise (we cannot "discover" something we have expected to find), and there is little surprising about conclusions that are available to common sense. Looked at more closely, most discoveries seem to possess a combination of destabilizing elements, which include (a) some unexpected phenomenon and (b) a displacement of awareness occasioned by this phenomenon in the discoverer's mind. Displacement of awareness might be termed "a state of quest"; under its influence, the discoverer rejects some element of previously accepted "reality" and seeks a new reality or gestalt that will accommodate the phenomenon that has been perceived.

During periods of quest, normal mental functions are distorted, much the way in which light is bent by a gravitational field. At least momentarily, the observer's mind is jostled out of the routine processing of routine subject matter, out of the normal progression of cause and effect. We might say that the observer's world suffers a temporary digression into absurdity or, to put it more poetically, that the veil of rational order is briefly lifted to reveal a more profound reality, paradoxical and almost dreamlike.

The momentary alienation from expectable realities is a time of fertility. Our usual attitude toward experience, built on assumptions and defended by rationalizations, is at most other times immune to discovery and resistant to nonconforming data. We walk by a fifty-dollar bill that lies on the sidewalk simply because *it ought not to be there*. But if the bill gets caught in an updraft and smacks us in the face — if the nonconforming data are highlighted by some unusual condition or element — we are more likely to take notice. We confront experience, briefly but dramatically, through a gap in our ignorance, a window in our preconceptions. We sense a liberation from the deadly constraints of self. We feel a power analogous to epiphany or poetic inspiration.

So it seems, at least, with minor discoveries. By extension, we may conjecture that major discoveries are made by people who are habitually alert to nonconforming data, habitually attuned to the little dissonances and coincidences of phenomena. These discoverers are sensitive to the poetics of experience: the process by which unusual phenomena suggest new images of nature. The state of quest is not something surprising to them, but rather a familiar state of mind.

Should discoverers, then, be wholly informal, thoroughly intuitive? Apparently not: for the only people who can be sure that data are nonconforming are those with a sure sense of form, and the only people who can justify their own intuitions are those who have the method to test and support them. In general, great discoverers seem to be so fully in control of method that method has all but ceased to be a drain on their awareness. Having internalized method, they may allow themselves the luxury of conjecture, the thrill of intuition. Having mastered order, they are open to the chaos of discovery.

THE PHILOSOPHY OF DISCOVERY

I have spoken of the material of discovery as nonconforming data, phenomena that do not jibe with our assumptions or conscious expectations. What are the chief characteristics of this material? Discovery, it would appear, normally occurs via the two main channels of cognition: analogy and anomaly. We are alerted to discovery by unexpected resemblances and unexpected distinctions.

Discovery by analogy. The analogies that inspire discovery are of two major kinds: interdisciplinary analogies, which link apparently disparate fields of experience, and intradisciplinary analogies, which establish new connections between elements within a single field of experience.

Interdisciplinary discoveries, in which individual modes and sometimes whole methodologies are imported from one field into another, are excellent examples of the phenomenon Koestler called bisociation. James Clerk Maxwell worked with interdisciplinary analogy when he established the interrelation between electricity and magnetism; Pythagoras was similarly impelled by analogies between number and sound. Fables and symbols and metaphors contain analogies by which artists and their audiences discover secrets about human reality and connections between various levels of experience. Early psychiatry used analogies between myth and psychology in developing the idea of the Oedipus complex; Carl Jung saw analogies between the symbolism of diverse cultures as suggesting a universal or "collective" unconscious. Interdisciplinary discovery by analogy is one of the most difficult of all forms of discovery, for deep similarities between diverse phenomena are often hidden beneath numerous superficial differences, while superficial similarities often lead researchers into absurd formulations.

Intradisciplinary discovery by analogy is usually based on some form of repetition. The repetition of similar events under differing circumstances creates a kind of analogy in time and suggests the presence of a unifying causal principle. Successful diagnoses of malaria and yellow fever were based on repeated connections between disease symptoms and the presence of certain varieties of mosquito. Cryptographers use repeated sequences of letters or other symbols in breaking codes. The grammarian Servius Maurus (c. A.D. 400), commenting on Virgil's repeated references to fire in Book 2 of the *Aeneid*, was perhaps the first critic to draw attention to the poetic device now known as imagery. A financial weekly announces that it can predict corporate takeovers by repeated dip-rise sequences in stock charts. Boxer A's corner notices that Boxer B always lowers his left hand before throwing a right. Because of its close relation with the most basic structures of learning, discovery through repetition is perhaps the most prevalent of all forms of discovery.

Common to all forms of discovery by analogy is the phenomenon of coincidence. Whether coincidences actually help researchers or, as happens more frequently, just distract them, they carry a uniquely dramatic and symbolic power. Perhaps this is because coincidence echoes from outside a psychologically internal creative process, a sudden connection between ideas that is common to both inspiration and discovery. Thus, if inspiration and discovery both involve mind imitating nature, coincidence is nature imitating mind.

Discovery by anomaly. While discovery by analogy comes through the unexpected perception of order and organization, discovery by anomaly is provoked by a disorganization of experience, not so profound as to throw us, like Lewis Carroll's Alice, into total confusion, but significant enough to challenge our current view of things. Having noticed the anomaly, we normally cannot rest until we have explained it in terms of our current view, or altered our view to accommodate it. To Thomas Kuhn, author of *The Structure of Scientific Revolutions*, anomaly is the very stuff of scientific progress, the catalyst for the renewal of thought systems. Discoveries of this sort fall into three major categories, which might be identified as follows: the anomaly of the uninvited guest, the anomaly of the empty chair, and the anomaly of rearrangement.

The anomaly of the uninvited guest. The discoverer notices the presence of an unexpected factor. About to sit down to dinner, Macbeth exclaims, "The table's full," not yet noticing that Banquo's bloody ghost completes the company. Through his new telescope, Galileo sees moons revolving around Jupiter — ocular evidence supporting Copernicus's attack on geocentricity. Henri Becquerel, having found that photographic plates lying near uranium sulfate crystals are unaccountably fogged, discovers radioactivity. Karl Jansky, hearing an unexplainable background noise on a powerful receiver, provides the basis for radio telescopy. Columbus's voyage to India is interrupted by the American continents. The anomaly of the uninvited guest is the most dramatic (though by no means the most prevalent) medium of discovery. Indeed, it is what most people think discovery is all about: that we discover by "coming upon" something that happens to be in our way. As most of my examples suggest, however, discoveries of this sort generally occur during the course of serious exploration or expert research.

The anomaly of the empty chair. This form of discovery, the exact reverse of the uninvited guest, is perhaps the most subtle and impressive of all those here described. In trying to account for or explain a phenomenon, the discoverer notices that a necessary factor is missing. This factor must then be supplied theoretically. Paracelsus, without palpable evidence of any kind, predicted the existence of bacteria. In particle physics, Paul Dirac's prediction of an anti-electron (subsequently called positron) and Wolfgang Pauli's prediction of the particle later known as the neutrino were based on the conviction that only the existence of such particles could explain the phenomena under study. Perturbations in the orbits of Uranus and Neptune led Percival Lowell to predict the existence and orbit of the planet Pluto.

As well as a medium of scientific discovery, the anomaly of the empty chair can be a means by which skilled writers inspire readers to make discoveries of their own. Some of Plato's dialogues (for example, the *Euthyphro* and the *Parmenides*) are deliberately left inconclusive: readers themselves must supply the conclusions suggested by the dialectic but absent from the text. Similarly, the haiku sets up a compressed structure of relations whose full significance must be "filled in" by the reader. Indeed, such discoveries in general demand a creative or "poetic" dimension in the mind of the discoverer. Such a combination of poetic and rational faculties occurs quite rarely in human nature.

The anomaly of rearrangement. In this medium the predicted factors are present but anomalously organized. Peter F. Drucker maintains that successful entrepreneurs are alert to anomalies in commerce and technology — situations, for example, in which accepted methods are not producing predicted results. The painter René Magritte was renowned for his skill in arranging familiar images into suggestive new structures: night foregrounds in day backgrounds, railroad trains emerging from fireplaces, human figures with heads of fruit. Few experiences are more anomalously organized than our own dreams, but inspired by these apparently chaotic phenomena, Sigmund Freud established the existence of subconscious psychological principles.

THE SYNDROME OF NONDISCOVERY

In limning the profile of discovery I have so far omitted the background of that profile, the negative forces that militate against our powers of discovery and discourage us from quest. Let us leave aside discussion of the most obvious negative factors: the depression, fear, and laziness that are so widely recognized as enemies of discovery, and the poverty and subjugation that are well known to be its political nemesis. We may go on as follows:

• People who try to please or otherwise gain acceptance seldom make important discoveries, for they limit their endeavors to contexts and channels that have been established by others. For this reason many academic fields in the humanities and social sciences, whose arguments are not scientifically demonstrable and whose denizens, therefore, are rewarded only when they have gained acceptance by respectable elders and specialized scholarly journals, are currently all but barren of real discovery.

• Conversely, rebels and mavericks driven by dissatisfaction and anger, however justified, generally make poor discoverers. To gain valid insights, we must love truth more than we hate error.

• Two sorts of fear can make discovery difficult or impossible. The first is fear of *discovery itself:* fear that the appearance of something radically new will endanger our own picture of reality or moral self-confidence or even sanity. The second sort is any fear at all that we hide from ourselves. Fear that is submerged, disguised, or otherwise bottled up inside us acts as a secret damper on whole areas of the mind. But fear honestly felt and openly expressed is a sign of mental health and may even aid in discovery.

• People deeply concerned about self-fulfillment and self-expression are often alien to discovery. Instead of seeing phenomena through limpid glass, they must look through their own reflected images. Discovery instead suggests the temporary immersion of subjectivity, the dissolution of the membrane that normally separates self from other. Similarly, discovery more often waits upon those who conceive of achievement as part of a communal effort than upon those who want it as a personal prize. The best-kept secret about real achievement is that it is synonymous with contribution.

• People will not discover much if they have strong "expectories" — that is, clear, sensible, forceful ideas about reality, which they project into the future as expectations. Such people are likely to be pretty successful in life. They will always be about 90 percent right about things: an average strong enough to take them far. But the 10 percent they miss will include all or most of the nonconforming data that lead to discovery. Such people ignore these data, or quickly dismiss and forget about them. The world they have built for themselves is too solid, too legal, to allow for change.

· Discovery is withheld from people who do not accept the simple operation of their own five senses as sources of continual pleasure and excitement. Seeing, hearing, and feeling are not passive functions but rather dynamic acts of will, steps in an evolving relationship between self and environment. People wishing to make discoveries must regularly evaluate, with new eyes, the phenomena of professional experience and the structures and sequences of everyday life. Failing in this creative ritual, they are blind to the subtle repetitions and minute innovations that suggest the influence of undiscovered principles.

· Because real discovery is based on subtle similarities to the past, or tiny divergences from expected forms, it is not available to people with poor memories.

· Nothing stifles the spirit of discovery more effectively than the assumption that miracles have ceased. In other words, most people do not make discoveries because they do not expect to. Discovery has in it not only exacting precision but absurd aspiration; it weighs hairs and expects miracles.

· Humorless people are unlikely to discover much. They are usually more concerned with their own dignity and rectitude than with anything going on around them. Unavailable to the sudden analogies and anomalies that cause laughter, they are apt to be dull toward other analogies and anomalies as well. Blind to their own humanity, they respond sluggishly to all other experience.

· Intellectually self-indulgent people make poor discoverers. By the intellectual self-indulgent, I mean people who develop mannerisms of inquiry or expression and cling to them through thick and thin. Granted, such mannerisms may at the outset bring confidence or even acclaim. But in the long run they will etch out a profile of limitations.

• Similarly, we must beware of the minor things that we do well. Specialized excellence has two dangers: that we will use it as a means of ignoring our own weak areas, and that specialized society will offer us excessive rewards for it, yoking us to plow a thin furrow. For these reasons, it is necessary to review and revise periodically not only the operations we do badly but the things we do best.

• Surprisingly, competitive instincts can impede our powers of discovery. When we compete with our local peers, especially with the purpose of making them realize that we are better than they, we limit ourselves to their models of expertise and end up, willy-nilly, playing their game. Competitiveness on a regional or national scale is less pernicious but still liable to analogous dangers. Even the fame won from successful competition can be an enemy of discovery, for fame is an unavoidable source of vanity and tends to erode privacy and limit free time. The goal of discoverers is not to outdistance their peers but to transcend themselves. Hence individuals bent on real achievement should not waste too much of their time succeeding.

While inspiration and discovery concern different areas of experience, they are similar at heart. Both carry the same rush of adrenaline, the same giddiness, the same temporary loss of identity. To achieve both inspiration and discovery, individuals must reconcile within themselves a number of classic dichotomies: knowledge and innocence, reason and emotion, conquest and surrender, subject and object, idea and matter. In quest of its own specific delights, the mind momentarily unifies these polarities of experience and, in doing so, transcends its own formalized and rationalized past and weaves new strands into the future.

4 Analysis

Integration, or even the word "organic" itself, means that
nothing is of value except as it is naturally related to the
whole in the direction of some living purpose.

— Frank Lloyd Wright, *Autobiography*

To this day I cannot read *King Lear,* having had the advantage
of studying it accurately at school.

— Alfred North Whitehead,
"The Education of an Englishman"

INSPIRATION AND DISCOVERY are not everyday experiences. But
as we have seen, they might never occur at all if it were not for
habits of mind that must be cultivated and renewed each day.
Such habits of mind become a kind of lens for interpreting daily
professional experience; additionally, they allow for the emotional openness that makes our experience exciting. These habits, moreover, are not usually the property of dreamers or misfits or dilettantes; instead they occur in people who have taken
pains to educate themselves in advanced professional functions and who make every effort to perform these functions
well.

So far, I have tried to show how such habits apply under unusual circumstances, in "charged" moments. Now I would like to discuss the way they apply to everyday work.

But how, in general, can we describe "everyday work"? Does the professional spectrum that includes executives, consultants, doctors, lawyers, scientists, professors, and civil servants involve any basic activity that is shared by all? In each of these professions, we must regularly evaluate new data and clearly express our conclusions about these data. Methods of evaluation and expression vary, but not by so much as to obscure their shared design. Such activities are informally known as "analysis," and, so conceived, analysis lies at the heart of modern professional enterprise.

Analysis is usually divided from such other workings of the mind as inspiration and discovery on the assumption that it operates according to a different set of principles. Analysts, we have come to believe, are cool, objective, and reductionist, if not downright mechanistic; while inspired individuals are intuitive and emotional, discoverers bold and impatient of detail. Categories of this sort are common in speech; they occur in educational programs, in which teachers are compelled to nourish this or that side of a child's brain or to emphasize one kind of "learning skills" at the expense of another.

I mean to question these divisions, not only by reevaluating current definitions but also by drawing attention to the many faculties and feelings brought into play in the analysis of art and nature. My aim is to show that, at its best, analysis is a creative process, an activity in which reason and emotion combine to open the mind to new discoveries.

FALSE MODELS OF ANALYSIS

The word "analysis" suggests conceptual difficulties. To analyze something (according to Webster) means to break it down into its constituent parts, or alternatively, to study something "systematically and objectively." These two definitions do not agree with each other, nor does either seem adequate in itself. Their combined inadequacy may be related to the fact that many analyses fail to do their job.

Look first at analysis as a "breaking down." When we analyze a Ciceronian oration, we begin by breaking it down into its structural components: exordium, narration, exposition, refutation, et cetera. When we analyze a rifle, we take note initially of stock, barrel, breech, sight, et cetera. These are valid procedures, but they are not enough. To separate something into its constituent parts is to risk losing sight of its external context. What was the occasion of Cicero's oration, and what sort of policy did it implement? What was his view of the relation between oratory, practical policy, and political philosophy? What are the uses of a rifle? What is its relation to other weapons? What is its significance psychologically, ethically, politically, historically?

When we ask about the causes or purposes of something, or about the inclusive category into which it fits, we are examining in effect the *outer face* of the subject; we are inquiring as to its position and its "shape." Understanding shape is important, not only because it can help us see the subject in its proper context but also because contextual circumstances can often determine internal structures. Frank Lloyd Wright's emphasis on "living purpose" and the natural relationship of part to whole is valid, not only in art and architecture, but in all the disciplines of understanding.

Failure to ask questions about context can result in absurd errors. We would not think much of a zoologist who studied the habits of house cats or chickens without considering the role that human influence had played in their evolution, or of a doctor who prescribed psychoanalysis to a prison inmate scheduled for speedy execution. Yet the modern world abounds with blunders that, though less obvious, are equally self-defeating. Lawyers concentrate on winning cases, judges on interpreting the law; but who in the system is directly concerned with justice? Science carefully and innocently provides the world at large with substances that the world at large routinely abuses. Medicine focuses on diseases and cures, frequently disregarding health. These and other such quaint atrocities pass unnoticed in modern society, often because they are aspects of the reductivism and specialization that are modernity's mother tongue. Far from being criticized as an error, the modern neglect for context is taken as a mark of professional competence.

And if analysis is merely reductive, what happens to the analogies and other connections that inevitably suggest themselves during the process of study? Reductivist analysts tend to dismiss such links and comparisons as unscientific and limit themselves to the safer processes of bifurcation and isolation. But hazardous as it may be, a sense of analogy seems to be an asset in a truly effective investigation. Could science have determined the unity of the electromagnetic field by reduction alone? What do we make of fractal constructs (for example, crystalline molecules) that are not only parts of a whole, but analogies to it? Would the development of analytic geometry, which projects equations into two- or three-dimensional space, have been possible without indulgence in analogies?

Analogy, as earlier described, is not just antireductive; it is also antiobjective. The Webster definition of analysis as "systematic and objective" fails to account for the mysterious nonverbal and even synesthetic avenues by which analogies come to us. Like the sense of context, the importance of analogy suggests that analysis is not a purely objective or logical action, but comprises the faculties of the whole mind. To analyze something in its full context, we need an understanding of the whole, a sense of goal and value. To profit from analogy, we need imaginative power and poetic receptivity.

If analysis, at heart, is neither an objective examination nor a breaking down, what may it be? In my opinion, real analysis is *exactly the opposite* of its dictionary definitions. Instead of being objective, true analysis is personal; instead of a breaking down, true analysis is a re-creation of a subject under study.

Subjects, after all, come to us as raw data: symptoms that suggest a specific disease, evidence that suggests a specific crime and criminal, bundles of reports that suggest specific market possibilities, lines of poetry that suggest a specific message. These data may be as mute and impoverished as the rubble from an explosion, or as confusingly abundant as the cellular population of a drop of blood. As the analyst internalizes these data, notes their interrelations, and tries various conclusions, the subject is no longer "raw" or alien but adopted live into the mind. And this living thing, if well nourished by memory, reason, and intuition, gives birth to a central idea. Our varied thoughts are suddenly parts of a unified, subsuming identity, a formal wholeness that justifies and gives new meaning to each of its parts.

The dynamics at work at these energized moments are paradoxical and dazzling. Momentarily, the distinction between subject and object completely dissolves, and both subject and object are enhanced.

The feelings that attach to this moment of apprehension are unmistakable. With relatively simple insights — like a schoolchild's discovery that what seemed to be an impossible mathematical problem is actually just an exercise in addition — there is a short flash of pure joy, a thrill as brief and perfect as the click of marbles on a rug. With greater insights there is the prolonged wonder, not so much of being wise oneself as of having stumbled into a wise world. The mind feels suddenly integrated with the power of nature and moves at nature's pace.

ANALYSIS AND WHOLENESS

Analysis thus would seem to have much in common with inspiration, discovery, and creative art. But if this is true, what of the traditional distinctions we make between "analytic" and "creative" pursuits? What of the boys and girls in school who show strong and exclusive leanings toward business or science or art? What of the boringly familiar character types of the dry, dogged scientist, the sloppy, expressive artist, the witty, fanciful writer? If the major civilized pursuits are so similar, what makes the pursuers so different?

The only answers to these questions that are consistent with the views just developed suggest a fairly comprehensive reappraisal of contemporary attitudes toward character and education:

Though our professional pursuits differ from each other, they would seem much less different if they were taught and practiced in the light of better theory.

Our children tend to develop narrow interests because our educational system does not adequately prepare them for the exercise of thought, and because our specialized and goal-driven society encourages them to develop professional strengths (as society perceives these strengths) rather than mental wholeness.

Most of our scientists and artists, writers and professors, fall into predictable character types, not so much because they have been isolated from all pursuits except their own, but rather because they have never fully come to terms with their own pursuits. They are not so much experiencing the fullness of science or art or literature as they are frozen in adolescent phases of professional development, replete with immature visions of science as divinely abstract, art as wholly unscientific, business as uncreative. Modern society rewards them for adopting these frozen postures because modern society needs specialized forces to achieve its short-term goals. Modern society, moreover, might feel less than comfortable with the formidable critics of its assumptions who might arise if the arts and sciences were more effectively taught and practiced.

ANALYSIS AND INVENTION

According to accepted theories, analysis (reduction to constituents) is the opposite of invention, which begins with constituents (material or abstract) and builds systems out of them. Now we are faced with the possibility that no such hard-and-fast distinction applies, and that in fact analysis is closely tied to invention. A focal point of good analysis, the apprehension of form, is arguably a creative act. A brilliant diagnosis or literary interpretation partakes of the same synoptic energy, the same ability to measure and balance and integrate heterogeneous data, that works in invention.

The relation between analysis and invention is nowhere more apparent than in one of the most effective analytic techniques: hypothesis. The hypothetical method is of a markedly creative character. In hypothesis, as in invention, a structure of ideas is modeled, sometimes almost from scratch, and given visible identity. In hypothesis, as in invention, the realization of this ideal structure depends on its exhaustive variety and its internal consistency. For all its vaunted practical effectiveness, hypothesis is a creative pursuit, an art form called into the service of science.

Conversely, art itself can be a form of hypothesis, the detailed elaboration and testing of an idea. Joseph Conrad stated that his great novel *Lord Jim* was an effort to exhaust the permutations of an idea, in this case the idea of "lost honor." Plato's dialogues (in which the idea of hypothesis originated) in general are complex definitions and testings of single ideas like "temperance," "virtue," and "justice." Many of Shakespeare's plays take ideas or connected sets of ideas and realize them on more than one plot line and on more than one level of meaning. Johann Sebastian Bach devoted profound attention to forms (passacaglias, fugues, variations, canons, and cantatas) in which single themes were subjected to brilliantly varied realizations or, if you will, to full analysis, while later composers, from Haydn on down, have achieved similar elaborations in the "development" section of the sonata-allegro form. A similar case could be made concerning major work in the visual arts, especially for "encyclopaedic" works like Michelangelo's Sistine Chapel frescoes and to artists like Turner, Monet, and Degas, who returned repeatedly to the same general subjects.

With regard to all these artists, and indeed with regard to art in general, it might be argued that the cornucopian faculty is responsible for the *exploratory* quality of aesthetic achievement. Again and again the quest for the fullness of an idea has led artists to revolutionary insights into phenomena natural and human. Without undue extension, the exploratory quality of art may be understood as having a character similar to well-practiced analysis.

To say all this is not to deny the very real differences between analysis and invention, and more generally between science and art as we know them. As I will try to show in a later chapter, art has its own goal, ancient, exclusive, and irreplaceable, though this goal has been obscured by time and change. My aim in these opening chapters has not been to demolish all the distinctions that separate our varied pursuits but to counter the false distinctions that tend to stifle communication among our disciplines and to obscure underlying continuities.

THE LIMITS OF ANALYSIS

Not every subject is open to analytic inquiry. To understand the type of challenge that defies analysis, we should look first at the general circumstances under which analysis is effective and then move on from there. I see two major types of "analyzable" challenges, which can be termed "Task" and "Problem." Beyond them, beyond the limits of analysis, lies an area we may call "Mystery."

CHALLENGE TYPE A: TASK

Suppose that some crucial message, some life-saving or life-renewing piece of information, lies embedded in a long text. The message, which is in the form of a Sunday magazine sort of cryptogram, is clearly marked on page 1453. We are fully aware of the significance of the challenge. Success depends on our skill in reading the cipher.

This situation exemplifies a broad range of professional challenges. Here are new data, suggesting new difficulty. But the nature of the challenge is clear to us, as are our resources for meeting it. A task is set before us, and all we have to do is determine whether or not our resources are adequate.

CHALLENGE TYPE B: PROBLEM

Suppose, again, that a message lies encoded in a text and that we are aware of the great importance of deciphering it. In this case, however, no further information about the challenge is available. We do not know where in the text the coded material occurs or exactly what sort of code is being used. In other words, we are uncertain as to whether the message can be found and (if found) as to whether our skill will be adequate to decode it.

Here the challenge is complicated by unknown factors. Where is the coded message? Is it a code we can deal with? Without preliminary research, we cannot define the nature of the challenge and hence are in doubt about the adequacy of our resources to meet it. Because of its unknown element(s), a Type B challenge demands a compound analysis, the first stage of which defines the difficulty and thus reduces it to the level of Task. The first stage of analysis can be called "diagnostic" and the second "therapeutic." Type B challenges are common across the professions, from laboratory science to land management, from pediatrics to literary interpretation. And though it may be somewhat patchy in teaching us what to do with the task when we have found it, professional education does distinguish between task and problem. Diagnostic skills are among the widely recognized goals of graduate schools and training programs. In general, the ability to deal with Type B challenges is what makes the difference between professional expertise and mere technical adequacy.

CHALLENGE TYPE C: MYSTERY

Once more, an urgent truth lies in a text. But no one has told us that it is there, much less that finding it is of paramount importance. Moreover, even if we have somehow turned to the correct page and are looking right at the message, there is no certainty that we will recognize it as a cipher, for it is written in language that, on the surface, looks exactly like everything else in the text. The only signal of a challenge, the only factor distinguishing us from the thousand readers who have examined the passage before us and found nothing, is a vague sense of disquiet: a sense either that there is something curiously "wrong" with the text or that there is something strangely wonderful about it. The only way to reduce this subtle code is by looking at language with new eyes, by radically reinterpreting what seem to be common and obvious verbal structures. And such a reinterpretation is impossible unless we are able, at least temporarily, to transcend our personal assumptions about language itself.

Here we have a special sort of problem, one so subtle and evocative that we may call it a mystery. Instead of an obvious challenge, there is a vague signal, a kind of uneasiness. The uneasiness is not localized; rather it hovers between ourselves and the subject in such a way as to blur the typical distinctions between subject and object. The normal analytic paraphernalia (terminology, methodology, use of historical precedent) are inadequate for this case, as are at least some of the assumptions and priorities we have carried into the situation. Rather than "use" our resources, we are challenged to transform them. Just as in some religious mystery that is set forth in texts and rituals but actually transacted in the subject's soul, we must, in solving the problem, solve ourselves. The result of such a solution is psychologically revolutionary. As Michael Polanyi puts it in a discussion of scientific discovery,

> Having made a discovery, I shall never see the world again as before. My eyes have become different; I have made myself into a person seeing and thinking differently. I have crossed a gap, the heuristic gap which lies between problem and discovery.

Mystery appears in many guises: as the disease that defies cure, as the faltering institutional system, as the ineffective ideology, as the persistent sense of failed opportunity, as the imperiled friendship. Mystery is so challenging as to be intolerable to some analysts, and so subtle as to be quite invisible to many others. Mystery (if I have defined it accurately) reveals itself to those who maintain an openness of character, or better (to quote André Maurois's biography of Disraeli), "a long youthfulness of heart." This youthfulness is a quality common to great achievement in all the disciplines. Its presence makes analysts susceptible to inspiration and discovery.

5 Imagination

Lorenzo de' Medici, to a friend who chided him for sleeping late: "What I have dreamed in one hour is worth more than what you have done in four."

— Baldassare Castiglione, *The Book of the Courtier*

IN LITERATURE and conversation the word "imagination" seldom appears but in the best of company. Artists are praised for it, schoolchildren are encouraged to develop it, and magazine ads suggest that major corporations have dedicated themselves entirely to its uses. Associated with total novelty, unbridled fantasy, historical progress, and political freedom, imagination is seen as a distinct faculty, capable of specific nourishment and separate function. Thus isolated, imagination is appealed to, by teachers and counselors, as some kind of genie that can be coaxed out of its bottle by specific pedagogical formulas or general clean living.

Closer scrutiny suggests a less romantic picture. "Imagination" is one of the vaguest words in the language, embracing everything from vain fancy to magisterial achievement. Using this word has the effect of boxing the mind into opposed categories (reason/imagination) that falsify the much more integrated processes of creative thought. Appealing to the imagination of one's children, students, or office staff thus tends to polarize their self-awareness in a rather unproductive way. For these reasons I have, perhaps perversely, managed to get through the preceding chapters without using the word once. On top of this, the mental operations we associate with imagination have gotten an undeservedly good press. Proceeding from the simplest possible definition — that imagination is the mind's capacity for conceiving of things that are not readily available through the senses — we may see imagination functioning in three ways. It can alleviate our psychological pressures by creating sleep-dreams and daydreams. It can help us achieve personal and professional goals. It can act as a free agent in contemplation, conversation, and pure mind play.

On the face of things, this scheme suggests that customary applications of the word "imagination" are somewhat flattering. Of the three activities of imagination, only the last suggests the kind of distinctness and liberty that are normally associated with the word "imagination," and this last level is arguably the least trafficked of all three. On the other tiers, imagination seems to function not as a solo voice but rather as part of an orchestrated effort — one in which it does not play a dominant role so much as respond to extrinsic necessities.

This subordination is clear enough in the sleep-dream, in which the imagination (as Freud teaches) serves as an unconscious mechanism of emotional catharsis. It is clear as well at the personal level, on which the imagination performs such necessary household chores as satisfying us as to the probable cause of a last-minute dinner invitation or telling us that a loved one's failure to return home on time is due to heavy traffic. It also applies on the professional level. Imagination in the service of a professional goal, even when that goal is deeply willed by the imaginer, is usually neither distinct from its context nor wholly free. Indeed, the pressures of goal dedication are often extreme and stifling enough to deter us from the very goals we seek.

The real test of "free" imagination, however, is the daydream. Given the customary view of imagination, we might expect the daydream to be an orgy of freedom, a fantasy touching upon a staggering variety of shapes and a limitless supply of topics. We might expect daydreamers to daydream that they are altogether different people, characters either chosen from personal acquaintance or created out of whole cloth. They might dream that they are not people at all, but rather specific real or imaginary animals, or forces of nature like storms or tides, or tables or clocks or steam engines. Casting off all physical limitations, they might dream that they inhabit a constellation of first principles or mathematical ideas, or that these very principles and ideas have changed to produce a delightfully eccentric universe.

But most daydreams are not like this at all. We daydream of ourselves *as ourselves;* we alter relatively few parameters and at that are rather conservative in altering them. We daydream not in miscellaneous fables but in universal, quasi-cinematic genera: the reliving or preliving of an emergency, the epic of glory, the sexual conquest, the idyll of riches. And it is the rare daydreamer whose daydreams, "free" as they are, do not include serious problems. The Nobel acceptance speech is crashed by protesters; the erotic feast is interrupted during hors d'oeuvres; the Rolls needs warranty work. As though uneasy in paradise, we pollute our visions with anxiety and shadow them with guilt.

None of this is very mysterious. Daydreams actually perform a function similar to sleep-dreams. They are seldom independent explorations or free initiatives. Their job is not so much to envisage new identity or transcend current limitations as to ease our frustrations about our identity and limitations. In daydreams, as in most other areas, our creative power acts as a responsive agent rather than a dominating principle. It is a kept genius, a Fitzgerald in Hollywood. It is fed and flattered; it is exploited and underprized.

But this is not all. In each of the processes described, imagination is conformist rather than revolutionary. In other words, it builds on preexisting assumptions about reality rather than questions them. This is so because in these processes imagination acts as an agent of equilibrium, a faculty that tries to bring what we perceive into balance with what we wish. Since what we perceive, as well as what we wish, partakes in large measure of our assumptions, imagination must adopt these assumptions, like the same old children's blocks kept in the same old basket, and make what it can with them. To be sure, it can reorganize these blocks, but it generally does not try to redesign them.

A working woman may imagine herself to be rich, but she does not imagine herself into a rich woman's boredom with money. An outcast boy may imagine himself popular, but he does not imagine the easy self-expressiveness and trust in human nature that popularity can bring. You can lie in your bed imagining yourself on a beach in Mexico, but you do not (that is, not without some practice) imagine yourself on that beach, missing the bed you lie in.

But suppose all this were reversed. The woman would daydream herself into a position in which, for the first time, she would be able to imagine herself, become aware of herself, as unconcerned with wealth. The boy might imagine himself into those personal qualities which, if thoroughly internalized, would make him popular. And you in your bed, suddenly wanting with all your heart to be precisely where you are, may know a moment of happiness.

Is such a reversal possible? I suggested that it was when I used the word "practice." Imagination can be free and edifying if it is taught certain habits. Scientists and artists learn these habits through the very nature of their callings: scientists in the development of their hypotheses, artists in the creation of their forms or fictions. In both good science and good art the mind must suspend its usual assumptions in order to meditate on something fundamentally new. In this process the mind is enfranchised; it surpasses itself. Good scientists and artists are what you might call lucid daydreamers. They free imagination from its psychic bonds and follow it on errands of truth.

A good fiction writer once told me that, instead of trying to "imagine" new stages in the plot of a story, she simply asks herself, "What happened then?" A well-known contemporary painter, in recounting the creation of his most famous canvas, tells us that he painted a small vase and then asked himself, piece by piece, what else was in the room. In both these artists, imagination is so strong that it seems to preside over its own shadow world, with a shadow history complete down to the last second, and shadow details accurate down to the last speck of dust.

These extreme cases suggest that the liberated imagination is a limitless faculty, heroically capable of redeeming life and renewing the world. They also suggest, however, that this faculty is not presented to us at birth, as a kind of free bonus to be turned on or off at will, but rather is a coordinate of other less dramatic strengths, fueled by commitment and developed over time. In fact, we see imagination as stemming from a psychological paradox similar to those described with regard to inspiration, discovery, and analysis: control and exuberance, precision and ambiguity, exacting professionalism and childish fun.

How can we encourage imagination in our children, our students, or ourselves? I suggest the following sample exercises with the caveat that, in my own experience, all have been difficult to implement and none has been sure of success:

With children. Tell children a story of your own invention that is long enough to stretch over several daily story periods. Establish in your story, insofar as possible, a strange cultural context. In this way you will be able, to some extent, to establish an alternate world with its own rules. It could, for example, be a world in which naughty children are rewarded for deeds of mischief, while good deeds are punished, or a world of water or a society of beings radically unlike ourselves. Pose problems and dangers in this world, and pause long enough during the narration to allow your listeners to imagine and suggest their own solutions. But remember beyond this that the most effective spurs to children's imagination are to congratulate them when they show it and to show it yourself.

With students. Assign two long-term creative projects, in the following order:

1. Ask students to design an ideal family home, keeping in mind that money is no object and that advanced drafting skills are not required. The home must fulfill the needs of all individual family members as well as those of the family as a group. No other requirements apply, except that the character of the home, from landscaping to decorations and appliances, must be highly detailed and justified in terms of its implications about the nature of family life.

2. Ask students to design an ideal but economically viable town, beginning with topography and street plan and proceeding, in a series of assignments, to parks, housing, commerce, education, and law. Require them to detail their choices in terms of their view of human nature and to take into account the potential consequences of their designs.

With self.

1. During free time, practice "unhooking" your consciousness from its normal schedule of worries, plans, memories, and daydreams. This may be done by a simple relaxing technique in which concentration on one of these topics, visualized as "work," is discarded in favor of nonconcentration, as "rest." This exercise may not positively strengthen the imagination, but it temporarily liberates the mind and makes it available to nonroutine possibilities.

2. Practice "fictional" daydreams in which you are a different

person (perhaps one of your family members or associates) or in which you live at a different time or in another nation.

3. Review your own activities and concerns in terms of new value systems, for example, (a) a system that prizes spiritual freedom above material achievement, (b) a system that evaluates lives and actions solely in terms of their humanitarian benefits, (c) the view of some jaded social scientist who sees all normal human activities as mechanistic responses to social stimuli, (d) a television director trying to market your life as a sitcom, or (e) the view of some future person attempting to piece together the details of your biography from existing records.

In planning these or other exercises, we should remember that the imagination does not receive full play unless it is called upon to reconstruct whole contexts of experience. The routine daydream, which usually alters specific details (for example, the type of car we drive, the amount of wealth we possess) rather than whole structures of experience, and the typical professional task, which has similar conceptual limitations, for this reason do not fully exercise the imagination. In order to function properly, the imagination must be rendered capable of remaking whole aspects of life, that is, of performing genuinely poetic or hypothetical operations.

The rationale behind these exercises is not that the imagination must be strengthened so that it may assist us in this or that mental task, but rather that, in and of itself, the imagination is an indispensable dimension of personality. Had we all the advantages in the world (that is, no need to fulfill tasks) we would still need imagination to enjoy our lot.

As I sit in my office, my radio reminds me of a topic I have missed. The disk jockey has just informed us that it is cloudy and probably drizzling. Outside there is not a cloud in the sky and the needle is edging 80. I think of the DJ, in her windowless studio, imagining the rain outside and feeling snug. Imagination can do little for people who are not alert to the world around them. Like a kite, which cannot fly unless strung to the ground, it has no power without ties to the "real" world conceived by us as accurately as possible. But its relationship to this world ought to be dynamic rather than subordinate. The strength of imagination lies precisely in its friction with a sense of reality that is equally strong.

Readers of Shakespeare will remember the whimsical and creative spirit Ariel, who delightedly obeys his master Prospero's behests yet continually pleads for his freedom. In Ariel we may understand the paradoxical nature of imagination: its blend of labor and liberty. This dualism is to be sought rather than avoided. Like some mentally stretched bow, it holds the vigor of the independent mind.

IMAGINATION AND MYSTERY

How can the imagination be applied to those special challenges which fall into the category I have called Mystery? Since inquiry into the mysterious presupposes the mind's ability to "reclassify" and reinterpret "familiar" information, the imagination might be expected to have a field day, questioning some meanings, ignoring others, reversing perspectives, altering parameters, and the like. That such victories so seldom occur testifies to a factor mentioned earlier in this chapter: the power that assumptions commonly have over the mind. Decoding mystery involves a step prior to imagination, a step in which the familiar is rendered unfamiliar, discharged of its ordinary associations and distinctions, its assumed reality.

William J. J. Gordon describes a procedure of this sort as "making the familiar strange" and sees it as allied with a converse procedure (making the strange familiar) in which the mind uses precedents and analogies to internalize and digest the new material. He states that his research

revealed that the most important element in innovative prob-
lem-solving was making the familiar strange because breakthroughs depend on "strange" new concepts by which to view a
"familiar" problem. For example, in the sixteenth century, people thought that blood flowed from heart to body, surging in
and out like the tides of the sea. Harvey [William Harvey,
1578–1657] was familiar with this view and believed it until he
closely observed a fish's heart that was still beating after the fish
had been opened up. Harvey looked for a tidal flow of blood,
but the action of the fish's heart reminded him instead of a
pump he had seen. The idea of the heart acting like a pump was
strange to him and he had to break his ebb and flow connection
to make room for his new pump connection.... Interdependent with the innovation process is the learning process where
one gains an understanding of a new problem or a new idea by
making the strange familiar.

Gordon goes on to show that making the strange familiar occurs when we use metaphor (heart/pump) to justify or symbol-
ize a new relation.

Gordon's views are strongly suggestive of what I have called
Mystery, but they do not speak fully to the challenge it seems to
represent. Take the example. Countless medically qualified observers before Harvey must have looked at countless beating
hearts, hearts whose beating did not seem "strange" to them in
the slightest. These observers must have assumed that the beating of these hearts was the consequence rather than the cause of
the ebb and flow of blood. In terms of the metaphor for mystery given in Chapter 4, these observers would have been like
readers looking directly at the coded message but not noticing
it because of its ordinary-looking language.

What these observers lacked, and Harvey had, was the ability
to find strangeness in a thoroughly familiar context. This ability, we must conclude, exists independently of the strangeness
or familiarity of external phenomena. It is perhaps best de-

scribed as the mind's capacity for making itself strange, for greeting phenomena with a set of shifting perspectives rather than seeing everything through the same rigid interpretive grid. Kaleidoscopic flexibility of this sort is what we need, not only in evaluating experiences that are genuinely strange or new, but also in newly seeing what is wonderful, or terrible, in day-to-day experience.

Such self-transformation is the most difficult and dangerous challenge to the imagination, and it is the most rewarding. Meeting it is possible only for the person whose mind is open to contradictions and well practiced in free conjecture.

One final conjecture of my own, which rightly belongs halfway between the end of this chapter and the beginning of the next: what we call imagination is deeply linked to what we consider beautiful. People who hate their work or fear it or are bored by it or treat it merely as an obligation are not likely to be very imaginative about what they do. What liberates the imagination is the sense that work in its theory and practice holds aesthetic possibilities, that jobs can be elegantly conceived and gracefully done. This sense of beauty unlocks feelings of pleasure and love that break down the barrier between worker and work and commit to work not merely the "thinking" consciousness but the full resources of mind.

6 The Sense of Beauty

Break the pattern which connects the items of learning and
you necessarily destroy all quality.

— Gregory Bateson, *Mind and Nature*

I OVERHEARD, in a university hallway, an exchange between two
students that went something like this:
"You won't believe what he [a professor of mathematics] said
in class yesterday."
"What?"
"He said there was really something called beauty."
"So?"
"I mean, not just a word or a feeling. He meant something
abstract, something permanent."
These comments illustrate some interesting aspects of our
intellectual climate. Over the past few decades, hard scientists and writers about the sciences have shown increasing interest in something that they call "beauty." This movement toward beauty seems to have little to do with sentimentalism;
rather, it appears to have emerged spontaneously from advanced research in highly visible fields. Scientific statements
about beauty, moreover, are not simply metaphors or teaching

devices; rather, they seem to be ways of describing a class of phenomena that will admit of no other definition.

Like most other scientific innovations, however, the discovery of beauty is greeted by the nonscientific community (here represented by the two students with the usual liberal arts undergraduate background) as something outlandish. Nonscientific Western culture, which has grown up in the backwash of nineteenth-century science, still generally assumes the materialist dogma (Marx, T. H. Huxley, Mach, and others) in which nature has nothing to do with such "conventional" human values as beauty. Nonscientific Western culture is about as ready to accept abstract beauty as it was to accept dialectical analysis in 425 B.C. or gravity in 1600.

But what did the mathematics professor mean when he referred to beauty? Did he mean something that can be isolated and examined, like gravity? Readers will forgive me if, instead of claiming that beauty can be isolated and examined, I remind them that gravity cannot. Unlike atomic energy or electromagnetism, gravity is not yet a documented and detailed physical presence (no one having yet proven the existence of a "gravity wave"); it is a useful supposition based on fairly accurate measurements of matter in motion. Because objects in motion behave consistently, and because no other known force can make them behave this way, we assume that they are obeying a single force, and give the hypothetical force a name.

From this point of view, beauty oddly resembles gravity: like gravity, beauty is a force whose existence is inferred from its apparent effects. You might even call beauty a kind of *spiritual* gravity, a natural force of attraction, cohesion.

Be this as it may, we may begin, rather cautiously, by describing beauty as a principle that is adduced from its distinct effects. But what are the effects beauty is supposed to produce, and what are the ways in which it does so? And what do beauty and its effects have to do with innovation and creativity? The last question should be answered first, because it calls forth the main premise of this chapter: Beauty and its effects are relevant to innovative vision because they seem to be the inevitable concomitants of any form, process, or idea that is truly seen. If the process of seeing, as suggested in chapters above, is always dependent upon the apprehension of wholeness, beauty may be described as a necessary dimension of wholeness. James Joyce wrote of a similar relation of ideas when, in the unfinished novel *Stephen Hero,* he discussed an experience he called "epiphany."

> First we recognize that the object is one integral thing, then we recognize that it is an organized composite structure, a thing in fact: finally, when the relationship of the parts is exquisite [here meaning, as in the Latin *exquirire,* "well searched out," with a pun on the normal meaning of the word], when the parts are adjusted to the special point, we recognize that it is that thing which it is. Its soul, its whatness, leaps to us from the vestment of its appearance. The soul of the commonest object, the structure of which is so adjusted, seems to us radiant. The object achieves its epiphany.

Joyce sees beauty not as a simple quality but as a function of the relation between subject and object. When a given object is properly understood (exquisite, adjusted), its beauty leaps out to the person who understands it. Beauty, therefore, is not a wholly independent force; neither, however, is it an illusion or social convention or mere "effect" of object upon subject. It is rather the natural and necessary consequence of the proper interaction between subject and object or, if you will, between mind and reality.

Key elements of this interaction underline the importance of beauty to scientific investigation and theoretical inquiry. What suddenly, in Joyce's words, "leaps to us" as "one integral thing" appears in the simplest possible terms. Simplicity is the byword of the current scientific discussion of beauty, as it is one of the perceived goals of modern scientific inquiry in general. By the simple, scientists do not mean the watered-down or made-easy; they mean wholeness without repetition or digression.

Wholeness, moreover, is coherent not only within itself but also in terms of its surrounding context, both in space and time. Beautiful things are not only suitable to themselves but also display fitness for the greater hierarchies that they inhabit.

Finally, inner coherence and contextual fitness invariably convey a sense of justice, or rather bring a moment when our moral consciousness expands beyond human affairs and into nature and the full arena of cognition. To the religious, natural beauty suggests divine wisdom; to the scientific, natural beauty suggests a pattern of nesting symmetries, at once global and profound, inhering both spatially and temporally. To some, these symmetries may in turn imply a natural justice, which at once validates human morality and transcends it.

If beauty results from our insight into the integrity or fitness of phenomena, what are the effects of such insight? We may describe two sorts of effect: pleasure and love. Pleasure is the passive effect of beauty, the receptive sensation that, at the moment of insight or recognition, expresses itself, complete with adrenal burst, in wonder or laughter or tears. Love, on the other hand, is the active effect of beauty: the will to repeat or increase pleasure by participating in beauty as fully as possible. Thus the people who are most capable of insight are most avid in their pursuit of chances to exercise it. More, perhaps, than by social reward, they are drawn into challenging careers by the sheer beauty that attends every discovery, by the innocent and undiluted pleasure of seeing.

This connection between the intellect and the emotions, between vision and love, was first documented by Plato. In the *Symposium* and the *Phaedrus* he discussed philosophy itself as an erotic activity, thus introducing the idea now inaccurately called Platonic love. In the *Symposium,* Plato describes the philosophical quest as a series of rising stages in which the erotic motive — the desire to participate in and enjoy beauty — grew more and more spiritual, until it focused on pure being and had little to do with physical beauty anymore.

For Plato the intensifying concentration on abstract beauty simultaneously makes philosophers themselves more beautiful in spirit. In the *Phaedrus,* he accounts for the inner transformation mythically as a purging of the impurities incurred by the soul in prior lives; but it can also be explained as a special version of the psychological toning that is inevitable in any healthy intellectual exercise. We cannot understand beauty without participating in it, or participate in it without subsuming its principles.

Plato's theory reflects an experience that we have all had in one way or another: the insight, gained from our own efforts or these combined with someone else's teaching, that fills us with unspeakable delight and seems to renew the world. This experience resembles other sorts of love in every respect except that it has no personal object or physical goal.

As a kind of intellectual eroticism, moreover, the enjoyment of beauty implies a unison of reason and emotion. When we experience beauty, reason and emotion operate reciprocally, conscious thought producing an emotional delight, which in turn impels it further. Properly developed, the sense of beauty imposes neither priorities nor distinctions between emotional and intellective impulses, but rather is open to both as partners in the search for form. By extension, we might characterize the insightful mind as a government that realizes that the quest for order (reason) is impossible without the guarantee of freedom (emotion).

All these premises suggest a rather surprising conclusion. If beauty is a necessary factor in a natural relationship, if it follows inevitably from the accurate perception of form, if it inspires pleasure and love, unifies reason and emotion, and provokes continued achievement, then all true education is education in beauty. Excellence of mind itself, rightly conceived, is expertise in beauty; creativity is wise love.

How can one sharpen one's sense of beauty? If beauty is indeed the concomitant of true insight into reality, of accurate apprehension of form, the sense of beauty can be developed through growth in the creative "habits" that have already been discussed. The frame of mind described in the early chapters — unbiased alertness to outer experience, readiness to review and alter prior assumptions, openness to inner promptings, unstinting study and practice — may offer the surest training in the appreciation of beauty.

What professional experiences are beautiful? How can a lawyer, say, or a tax accountant, experience beauty in the course of work? Every professional field — indeed, every field that demands individual inventiveness — offers opportunities for the flash of insight described with relation to Joyce and Plato. Beyond this are all experiences involving justice. Human justice, which might best be described as a kind of symmetry in time, resembles the natural symmetries and reciprocities that strike us as beautiful. To speak or act justly is to create a symmetry between self and experience. Thus fairness is beautiful, because it suggests a symmetry between what people deserve and what they get. Frankness (in measure) is beautiful, because frankness equates what we say with what we feel. Humor is beautiful, that is, when humor can convey elegantly and creatively things that are impossible to put frankly. Precise expression of any sort has beauty because of the symmetry between reality and the signs that convey it. In short, anyone who performs difficult tasks inventively, justly, and with humane expressiveness works in the presence of beauty.

The almost universal relevance of beauty has philosophical implications as well. Since beauty is an aspect of all accurate perception, regardless of field, we may see it as a bond connecting all fields and revealing, beneath apparent distinctions, the latent unity of thought. Students who recognize the aesthetic dimension of all inquiry better understand the ways in which all fields and studies are part of an integral human project, an enterprise coherent in its standards and goals. They realize that the aesthetic values that inhere in all disciplines also inhere, on a different level, to the philosophical relations between the disciplines, to the political contexts in which the disciplines operate, and to the historical matrix in which they have developed.

Aesthetics, in other words, can assist us in uncovering links not only between mind and nature, but also between the scientific, humanistic, and political professions, between past, present, and future. For Gregory Bateson the perception of beauty could make us aware of a "pattern which connects the items of learning." Rightly studied, aesthetics can newly establish such a pattern, or restore one that we have lost.

But what of ugliness? I can imagine a professor — not a mathematician this time, but maybe a zoologist — challenging his or her students to find anything in nature that is truly ugly. The professor might assert that there is nothing ugly in nature, that all natural phenomena have in space/time that combination of wholeness and fitness that would strike the careful interpreter as being beautiful.

Such an argument can be continued as follows: Ugliness is a human artifact, not only because it is an illusion that human beings sometimes project upon nature, but also because it is a term accurately applied only to human actions. Aggressive, inventive, lacking at once the wisdom of gods and the instinct of beasts, human beings are uniquely capable of actions that are neither whole nor fit, initiatives that lack beauty in time and space. Ugliness, in other words, is a corollary of human freedom.

This explanation would have analogies in the implication of

Genesis that Adam and Eve were expelled from Eden (grace or perfect nature) because they knew good and evil (had free choice), and in the once-influential Neoplatonic view that humanity alone has a moral status that is not determined by nature. Our freedom and indeterminacy make us capable of the worst as well as the best; we are at once the only beings able to produce ugliness and the only beings able to appreciate beauty.

This paradox has important bearing on the development of the sense of beauty. It ensures that our perception of beauty will almost always be hampered by the unbeautiful accretions of culture: the vain systems of pedants, the din of the mass market, the wreckage of cynicism, the poverty of common sense. Our aesthetic life is weakened not only by the admitted uglinesses of culture but also by its pretended beauties and truths.

Such culture-bound beauties and truths inevitably acquire theoretical spokesmen who create a kind of *ethics* of beauty: a paradigm specifying what is to be seen as beautiful and what is not. In the wisdom of the accepted paradigm, beautiful insights and beauty itself may be dismissed as ungainly and ugly. This potentially tragic injustice, which has an important bearing on the moral character and political consequences of creativity and innovation, will be discussed in later chapters.

You may think it strange that I have gotten through all this talk about beauty without once using, as example, something I think is beautiful. What an opportunity I have missed: to weave into my words a garland of poems, paintings, equations, and mystifying Chinese aphorisms. In response to this, the best I can do is suggest that you reread this chapter while listening to a good performance of Monteverdi's *Vespers* of 1610 or Mozart's Mass in C Minor. Beauty can't be triggered by a few words of reference; it must be recreated each time it is to be experienced.

Nonetheless, I mean to leave you with something beautiful. It is not a creation of genius but a few words spoken by someone long dead and recorded by a man who was profoundly capable of appreciating them. These words are not only a thing of beauty in themselves but an object lesson in how beauty is perceived.

As a young man, the psychiatrist Viktor Frankl was deported to Auschwitz. His medical background made him useful to the authorities, who employed him to attend the sick and dying. Among the many stories he tells of those times is one that serves for him as a special example of "inner greatness." It concerns someone who was fatally ill.

This young woman knew that she would die in the next few days. But when I talked to her she was cheerful in spite of this knowledge. "I am grateful that fate has hit me so hard," she told me. "In my former life I was spoiled and did not take spiritual accomplishments seriously." Pointing through the window of the hut, she said, "This tree here is the only friend I have in my loneliness." Through that window she could see just one branch of a chestnut tree, and on the branch were two blossoms. "I often talk to this tree," she said to me. I was startled and didn't quite know how to take her words. Was she delirious? Did she have occasional hallucinations? Anxiously I asked her if the tree replied. "Yes." What did it say to her? She answered, "It said to me, 'I am here — I am here — I am life, eternal life.'"

In this story beauty and creative insight are so thoroughly mingled that it is hard to say which gives rise to the other. Beauty functions on two levels: the nameless woman's sense of the tree in bloom as a symbol of continuing life and Frankl's recognition of the greatness implicit in what she felt and said. On both levels the perception of beauty is tied to transfiguring insights: the woman's inspired sense of belonging to a life that will transcend her own body's and Frankl's sudden realization that the woman is not delirious but inspired.

These insights, focused in the reader's mind by Frankl's simple narrative, generate a third kind of beauty, something that might be called a beauty of sudden seeing. We are suddenly aware that something we had thought impossible is radiantly clear; we are thrilled by an unexpected amplification of mind. Frankl's story shows the deep connection between creativity and the perception of beauty and illustrates many of the premises about creativity developed in these early chapters. Both the young woman and Frankl reached new awareness through a painful confusion that was followed by the perception of wholeness and form. Both reached awareness through an emotional torment, honestly and bravely suffered, that gave way to transcendent fulfillment. The basis of this fulfillment was a single metaphor, tree = life, the creative act of a mind expanding into its environment and expressing a massive continuity of energy and form.

To this point I have tried to show how the recognition of such continuities is essential in all forms of creative activity, from inspiration to analysis. In chapters to come I hope to show how the sense of wholeness can bind creative people to their society and how, paradoxically, it can alienate them from it.

PART II   *The*
            Ethics
            of
            Creativity

7 *Introduction*

WHEN THE MONK wisely counseled young Michel Colombe to learn "the grace of great things," he drew a connection between ethics and creativity that was more than merely metaphorical. The word "grace," and the pattern of moral strengths that it suggests, are profoundly relevant to major creative achievement. They are relevant not only on the social level, on which creative people interact with their peers, but on the individual level, on which prolonged achievement can depend on the cultivation of a heroic, even philosophical attitude toward one's own work.

The five chapters that follow will chiefly concern the first of these levels: the moral values suggested by individual creative activity. As we have already seen, creative achievement suggests qualities of character — openness, precision, self-discipline, self-scrutiny, love of form and beauty — that have significant ethical implications. This is not to say that all great artists have led beautiful lives or that all major scientists have been superbly rational parents and citizens. Rather we may say that creative people take an especially serious attitude toward their work and tend more than others to conceive of this work in value-laden terms: to project moral consequence into actions that other people would see from a merely technical or economic perspective. This phenomenon would account for the moral content (the use of words like "justice," "validity," "propriety,") in the language of nonmoral disciplines like mathematics and the natural sciences. Alfred North Whitehead expressed the relationship between creativity and ethics succinctly when he asserted that "style is the ultimate morality of the mind."

What is the ethics of creativity? Our first impression is one of strangeness. Indeed, when I compare creative values with other moralities, I am reminded of a Lewis Carroll fantasy or of scientific fields — surface chemistry, for example, or quantum theory — in which certain common assumptions about the way nature behaves do not apply. Our own inherited moral assumptions, a belief pattern based on the exigencies of social interaction in a modern urban world, have little meaning to the creative mind. This is not to say that the creative mind is "amoral"; its rules in fact seem uncommonly stringent. I mean rather that, particularly in key moral areas like pain and pleasure, courage and integrity, the distinction between "self" and "other" and the idea of freedom, creative experience redefines basic parameters so radically that we seem to be entering a new moral universe.

The psychologist Abraham Maslow eloquently describes this world in terms of the fusion of opposites. Creativity, he suggests, develops a new morality by transcending long-held distinctions like those between reason and instinct, wish and fact, hedonism and altruism, childhood and maturity. These polarities, massively immovable in normal ethical experience, are obliterated by a global creative energy, an uncompromising concentration. Character is temporarily reunified, reconstituted as the agent of a single act of will.

This metamorphosis confers a double benefit. Creative activity not only introduces us to a new set of values but provides us, as a kind of by-product, with a new perspective on the conventional values that we have inherited. Insight into the ethics of creativity suggests that our own basically liberal ethos, though tried and true, is neither the only possible ethos nor, in its present condition, the most viable one. Paradoxically, liberal assumptions can sometimes discourage creative achievement; thus it is incumbent on liberalism to develop a self-critical faculty that will render it at once hardier and more amenable to innovation.

For these reasons the ethics of creativity, as it regards an individual's own creative enterprise, verges on and blends into the broader social sphere. There are other reasons as well. The product of creative achievement is always some form of power, ranging in extent from the power to support or destroy whole civilizations to the power to make a single listener laugh. Some forms of new power — for example, weapons or sources of energy — are "loud" or easy to recognize; other forms — for example, medical breakthroughs or advances in the treatment of information — are "quiet" but may be equally epoch making. Power always has ethical implications, and those who produce it are to some extent accountable for the uses that are made of it. New power, in particular, suggests ethical complexity because it implies conflict between the innovator and the proprietors of established power sources. Though these social topics are more properly the subject of Part 3, they will unavoidably crop up in the section that follows.

8 Integrity

There was never a sound beside the wood but one,
And that was my long scythe whispering to the ground.
What was it it whispered? I knew not well myself;
Perhaps it was something about the heat of the sun,
Something, perhaps, about the lack of sound —
And that was why it whispered and did not speak.
It was no dream of the gift of idle hours,
Or easy gold at the hands of fay or elf:
Anything more than the truth would have seemed too weak
To the earnest love that laid the swale in rows,
Not without feeble-pointed spikes of flowers
(Pale orchises), and scared a bright green snake.
The fact is the sweetest dream that labor knows.
My long scythe whispered and left the hay to make.

— Robert Frost, "Mowing"

WHAT HAS CREATIVITY to do with integrity? One possible answer lies in Robert Frost's strange line, "The fact is the sweetest dream that labor knows." Labor, the line tells us, is its own reward, because only labor evokes "the earnest love" that can see, in "the truth" or "the fact," beauties more thrilling than the stuff of dreams. Frost suggests to us that a by-product of work well done is a kind of integrity, a sense of wholeness in which worker, tools, and product are linked together and mutually fulfilled. In particular, his poem speaks profoundly of the focused commitment and delight in labor that mark the creative mind.

How may "integrity" be defined more specifically? We may best begin by looking at the word as it is commonly used. Ironically, "integrity" is a strangely hollow word. Of all the major ethical nouns in English, "integrity" alone lacks a concomitant adjective, neither "integral" nor "integrated" adequately conveying its meaning. It is a kind of orphan noun, a word untranslatable into practical terms. Apparently, though our culture likes the idea of integrity, we have felt uncomfortable about conferring it on people or actions as a positive characteristic.

Hollowness is suggested as well by the extent to which the word is taken for granted and by the narrow and arbitrary meaning that is normally assigned to it. "Integrity" is thrown around by journalists who assume that its meaning is obvious, and it is employed like a bludgeon by political and religious interests. People of "integrity," all assume, rise and retire early, make painful sacrifices, drink milk, don't joke about serious matters, and never need to wash their underwear. Such assumptions explain why so many public figures who are regarded as having integrity seem stubborn, moralistic, or simply washed out. By extension, they also explain why so few people of outstanding ability seek public office in modern democracies.

With these misgivings in mind, we would be justified in rejecting what the word "integrity" seems to mean and inquiring as to what, seriously considered, it *has* to mean. Only three definitions of the word would seem able to survive analytic scrutiny, and these meanings must be understood as complementary and interdependent. Integrity is

1. an inner psychological harmony, or wholeness;
2. a conformity of personal expression with psychological reality — of act with desire, of word with thought, of face with mind, of the outer with the inner self; and

3. an extension of wholeness and conformity in time, through thick and thin. Though integrity can be, and must be, expressed in individual actions, it is not fully realized except in terms of continuity.

Thus understood, integrity may be defined as psychological and ethical wholeness, sustained in time.

Admittedly, this working definition is imperfect and needs some adjustment. What about a person who is innerly and outerly, now, then, and forever, perverse or bitter or dull? Should we speak of a guileless slob, a self-acknowledged worm, an unrepentant rat, as having integrity? Should we include as well the milk-drinking moralists of current fame? To understand why none of the above qualify, we must look back to the words "wholeness" and "expression" in definitions (1) and (2). These words preclude arbitrary behavior, whether moralistic or immoral. They preclude the dull and the dense, the formulaic and the simplistic. They suggest instead a person at ease with and open to inner promptings of spirit, both simple and complex. They suggest uninhibited passage, from thought to action, of native mental energy.

Similarly, if integrity means a kind of uniformity in time, what is the difference between integrity and mere stubbornness or lack of discretion? Is Shakespeare's Hotspur, who behaves almost identically toward his king, his wife, and his horse, a model of integrity? Clearly the word cannot be spread so thin. Integrity presupposes discretion: for one's sense of the "good" must necessarily include a sense of the appropriate, by which one modifies one's words and actions in response to discrete stimuli and changing situations. What, then, separates the person of integrity from the pragmatist? Only, we must reply, that this "sense of the appropriate" must conform to inner harmonies as well as outer circumstance. A person of integrity can alter the tone, but not the tune.

Finally, what about the "painful sacrifices" so often associated with lives of integrity? What of the writer who turns down a six-figure Madison Avenue job in order to publish the truth? What of the nun who devotes a lifetime to healing sick children? The answer is embarrassingly simple. Given the "wholeness" and "expressiveness" characteristic of integrity, these are not sacrifices at all, but acts of fulfilled intention and unified will. They imply pain or self-denial only to the extent that we, as onlookers, project upon them our own disunified sensibilities. Rather than sacrificing happiness for the good, the monarch and the nun would seem to be sacrificing lesser pleasures for greater ones.

Integrity, thus understood, is not a painfully upheld standard so much as a prolonged and focused delight. The psychologist Abraham Maslow calls such delight a form of "self-actualization"; describing a group of creative people at work, he concludes,

> My subjects had put opposites together in such a way as to make me realize that regarding selfishness and unselfishness as contradictory and mutually exclusive is itself characteristic of a lower level of personality development. So also in my subjects were many other dichotomies resolved into unities, cognition vs. conation (heart vs. head, wish vs. fact) became cognition "structured with" conation as reason and instinct came to the same conclusions. Duty became pleasure, and pleasure merged with duty. The distinction between work and play became shadowy. How could selfish hedonism be opposed to altruism, when altruism became selfishly pleasurable? These most mature of all people were also strongly childlike. These same people, the strongest egos ever described and the most definitely individual, were precisely the ones who could be most easily ego-less, self-transcending, and problem-centered.

In this regard, Maslow would have enjoyed the two stories that follow. The first was told by Charles Darwin about his early life.

But no pursuit at Cambridge was followed with nearly so much eagerness or gave me so much pleasure as collecting beetles. It was the mere passion for collecting, for I did not dissect them and rarely compared their external characters with published descriptions, but got them named anyhow. I will give a proof of my zeal: one day, on tearing off some old bark, I saw two rare beetles and seized one in each hand; then I saw a third and new kind, which I could not bear to lose, so that I popped the one which I held in my right hand into my mouth. Alas it ejected some intensely acrid fluid, which burnt my tongue so that I was forced to spit the beetle out, which was lost, as well as the third one.

This story is a dramatic example of what I mean by integrity. Notice that young Darwin has no particular goal in mind; it is the "mere passion for collecting," the urgent purposeless delight, that drives him on. His little deed of heroism in popping a live insect into his mouth is not the act of a crusader who consciously undergoes discomfort in the service of a higher end. Neither is it the hardiness of a soldier who has learned to endure pain as a conditioned reflex in the cause of duty. It is rather the impulsive expedient of a person caught up in the simple joy of action. The total absorption of character and pureness of intent — the integrity — is exclusively a function of his joy.

The second anecdote is somewhat more wholesome. David Herbert Donald recounts the following incident from the novelist Thomas Wolfe's early travels in England with his friend Aline Bernstein:

Along the way, at Ilkley, Aline made a most practical contribution to Tom's career as a writer: she bought him three sturdy ledgers, bound in red cloth. Years later, he naively called this purchase "one of the most important events in my life as a writer." Writing in these big ledgers "gave me joy and hope," he observed with a note of wonderment; "I could no longer lose the pages, because they were bound together."

Was Wolfe's comment really naive, or is the biographer missing something essential in the story he tells? Wolfe's joy and hope at the sight of the three ledgers are like young Darwin's magnificent concentration at the discovery of the three beetles: in each case the discontinuities of normal consciousness have fallen away and the full resources of mind are focused on a single idea. For Thomas Wolfe, with his emotional energy and strong sense of symbol, the ledgers were more than tools or toys. They represented, in a way that nothing else could, the future act of writing, the future embodiment of a work of art. The idea of his future work, immaterial yet urgent, was evoked and given fullness by the large and strongly bound ledgers.

In our own barren sophistication, our own distance from such an awareness, we may call his wonderment simple-minded; more rightly, it should be considered an expression of profound understanding. To ignore or misinterpret such expression in others or ourselves is to neglect the integrity of the creative awareness; it is to overlook the wisdom of delight.

THE HABITAT OF INTEGRITY

SITUATION AND ATTITUDE

Can such wisdom be learned? Having counseled many writers, I can attest that, though difficult, it is possible. I call in evidence a single case study, drawn from the life of a woman I will call Camilla.

Forty-five years old, married, and the obsessively devoted mother of three, Camilla had worked for some years as a university instructor in literature. Though she had been a highly promising student and was known as a gifted teacher, Camilla had never made much progress in what she considered the most challenging and rewarding branch of her profession, the publication of research. Ideas abounded, but when she sat down to express them, she immediately felt a variety of bad vibrations, including confusion, doubt, depression, distraction, and self-anger. In annoyance, she would postpone or avoid her work, acts rewarded inevitably by waves of guilt. And when guilt drove her back to the typewriter, annoyance would drive her away again.

All this, she told me, had gone on for years.

One summer three things happened that radically altered Camilla's situation. She won a grant enabling her to attend a six-week seminar in her own field of research on a distant campus. Her husband agreed to stay home with the children while she attended. He set up a word processor for her in her office while she was away.

The seminar was a marathon academic jam session, excellently directed; the participants were enthusiastic and mutually encouraging.

Camilla came home full of energy and resolve. She set out at once to master word processing from scratch, and simultaneously began decorating her office with posters and plants. In a week she was writing, not out of guilt or obligation, but with a sense of exhilaration and self-expression. She has not stopped since.

This is admittedly a rare example. Most of the people I have counseled have been unable to separate (as Camilla did) work from obligation and to align it with pleasure. I can teach students endless details about the technique of writing but never infuse in them the joy that makes everything come to life. But rare though it may be, Camilla's experience can teach us something about the origins of creativity. At the risk of oversimplifying, let me list the forces that operated in her case.

1. Praised for her work both as student and teacher, she had a mental precedent of her own excellence.

2. She had suffered long and honestly, without blaming anyone but herself; she was "rich" in failure and ready to break through.
3. Winning the grant reawakened her sense of self-worth.
4. Her husband's success as a single parent freed her of her feeling of indispensability to her family.
5. The distant seminar put her in a completely new role and context, thus establishing a matrix for her own renewal.
6. The seminar demonstrated memorably the results to be achieved from uninterrupted concentration on a single subject.
7. During the seminar work became identified with pleasure (a pleasure prolonged symbolically by Camilla's decoration of her office).
8. Seminar participants offered each other intense peer encouragement.
9. The word processor brought new freedom for rapid composition and revision, as well as a sense of professional independence.

Most of these vectors arose from changes in Camilla's environment. Such changes, though far from being everyday occurrences, are not impossible to duplicate, in Camilla's or other creative fields. Seminars like the one she attended, designed to bring the sort of renewal she achieved, are available in many professional areas. All that was truly unusual was Camilla's attitude. She had fought writer's block gamely and with no illusions as to its cause. She took responsibility for her own failures and knew, conversely, that no one but she could reverse them. She stood on the threshold of integrity, and needed only a nudge to get there.

By extension, Camilla's honesty and its rewards are reminders that intense involvement in creative work, or any other worthwhile aspect of life, is facilitated by an honest attitude toward oneself and one's surroundings. Frost's statement, "The fact is the sweetest dream that labor knows," can be applied to creativity, when a career of achievement can depend on the unflinching acknowledgment of a few simple facts. The simplest, the one most central to creativity, is that we are personally responsible for most of the major events in our lives and for all our responses to these events. Recognition of this fact opens up a vision of human reality that is at once vivid and durable. In addition, it relieves us of the strain occasioned by the excess baggage of self-excusing fictions.

PROFESSIONS, DEMOGRAPHICS

How does integrity function in professional life? Apparently, first of all, in one's choice of a profession. It is said of the Himalaya, that beautiful and profoundly challenging environment, that "the mountains choose their people." You can say something similar about the professions. Between the extremes of the philanthropic and disinterestedly creative pursuits on the one hand, and narcotics sales and arms traffic on the other, you may plot a curve on which each profession, as demanding more or less integrity, has a general location.

We associate integrity with artists, inventors, solitary masters, individuals who are completely in command of their professional careers. Whether or not this is accurate in individual cases, the general idea seems valid: integrity is fostered by a sense of independence and by the ability to see one's work through from beginning to end. Conversely, principles unfriendly to wholeness are impersonal corporate structures or the failure by employers to delegate responsibility to employees and the division of labor and the divorce between process and product.

The first of these factors has, for many years, been the object of passionate but ultimately fruitless attacks. Indeed, the modern critique of corporate dehumanization has much in common with the critiques of bureaucracy mounted generations ago by Dostoevski and Tolstoy. Such outcries offer spiritual consolation but do not change the system. Corporate organisms, which respond poorly to sermon or decree, do not change until it becomes apparent in the plainest terms that companies which encourage creativity and responsibility at every personnel level fare better than those which do not. And a realization of this sort, however valid, is unlikely ever to break upon executives who are more interested in annual figures than in long-term development.

The second factor is apparent in two complementary phenomena, process without product and product without process.

Process without product: professional piecework, committee work in which sections of a project are assigned to individuals, high school or college teaching in which the same pie wedge of learning must be served up, year after year, to class after class. Such careers develop relatively narrow talents and discourage holistic thinking. Unless they are leavened by self-knowledge, they become psychological prisons whose effects grow more damaging as people grow more comfortable in their confines.

Product without process: automated kitchens, greeting cards with printed messages, ski lifts, snowmobiles, golf carts, guided tours. Here the natural role of work is eliminated from the process of achievement. The apparently desired goal is served up without fuss or sweat, but divorced from the labor of attainment, it may seem hollow, almost prostituted. In a vacuum of process, goals can never be satisfying and tend to grow tedious.

Such theories of integrity have analogies in other forms of day-to-day experience. Life among huge crowds does not encourage a sense of individual identity; conversely, life without love and communication drains our sense of communal human identity. And efforts (encouraged by a variety of pills and gadgets) to deny our own physiological reality in the name of comfort often obliterate that form of self-knowledge which concerns our place in nature. Commuting long distances, aside from fatiguing us and wasting time, destroys spatial integrity, the sense of our particular environment as an extension of personal character. Moreover, commuting promotes the establishment in individuals of separate geographic "selves" — in other words, of people who automatically switch value systems when moving from one locale into another.

Forms of demographic integrity vary with the character and profession of the individual involved. The type that I personally know and like best can be found in my hometown, Eugene, Oregon, and a number of other medium-size cities in the Northwest. Dwellers in such cities are never far from nature and can carry on the business of life without being harried or cramped. The weather is temperate. There is relatively little crime, poverty, crowding, demagoguery, profiteering, pollution; people are spared the incessant racket of jet aircraft engines; they can live on locally grown food and often buy it from the growers; their town was laid out with human nature in mind and is so maintained; they can look out urban windows up tree-lined streets into fields and mountains. Metaphorically, we might say that their environment is a macrocosmic image of them as individuals, because it not only satisfies their needs but embodies their aspirations. As such it is radically different from other urban environments (New York, Las Vegas, Los Angeles) that satisfy some needs and deny others, that overly indulge some aspirations and categorically suppress others.

Environments like Eugene encourage a state of mind in which people can enjoy a variety of experiences — work, education, leisure — without huge shifts in psychological tone. Moving easily from rest to work, from business to friendship, the dweller in such an environment can go through daily life as the same person, rather than a constantly adjusting defense system. And because of these factors, personal life in such an environment can be seen not as a more or less successful response to circumstance, but as a willed process.

The life of integrity may thrive on contraries: work and rest, action and contemplation, mental and physical, laughter and tears. But it does not thrive on contradictions. In particular, it cannot exist in environments in which basic contradictions, rather than being recognized as such, are unconsciously accepted as necessities of life.

CHRONOCOSM: THE INTEGRITY OF TIME

No matter where we live, we inhabit the continent of time, a continent less studied and charted than any other. Creative people move purposefully across this continent, truly explore it. The rest of us shack up in little patches and clearings of time, always harried, always distracted, slave to the next knock on the office door or phone call. Our professional lives show an alarmingly high percentage of "response activities" — meeting deadlines, obeying directives, dealing with emergencies — as opposed to activities developing independent initiatives. Even sophisticated professionals — doctors, lawyers, scholars — face cycles of deadening repetition. Our homes are parceled out into service spaces (kitchen, bath, bedroom) and social areas (living room, dining room), with little or no space set aside for productive initiatives or private contemplation.

Creative activity demands the opposite. The protected, and usually large, physical spaces that creative individuals demand for their work — studios, libraries, laboratories — are matched by the protected expanses of time that they stake out, day after day, across their careers. These regularly repeated periods, often whole mornings or afternoons, are so massive that they become quasi-physical presences whose substance can be sculpted into regular achievement. I call these expanses of time "chrono-cosms" (time worlds): periods that set up their own unique time dynamics, develop an integrity all their own. People unacquainted with such time worlds have little chance to experience creative insight.

INTEGRITY AND SOCIETY

While the simpler forms of integrity (for example, the frankness and exuberance of early childhood) are indulged and praised by society, more sophisticated forms of integrity inspire malice as well as admiration. The image of people delightedly involved in life is an annoying reminder to onlookers that they themselves are not.

People of integrity, moreover, tend to develop and support strong positions on issues of general concern which, if they diverge enough from our own, may threaten our moral security. If they agree with us, the threat can be even more severe. The unembarrassed statement of our own principles implies distressingly that we may have to put our own bodies on the line for them. Indeed, if there is anything more bothersome than an open affront to our shared values, it is a strong statement of them.

Those disturbed by integrity have easy ways of taking revenge. Because it always deviates from popular modes of behavior, integrity can always be made fun of. People of integrity are vulnerable to derision because they do not wear the uniform, to exclusion because they tend to forget the password. They are an easy mark for caricature because their wholeness looks asymmetrical to the prevailing astigmatism. Nor can they be counted on always to respond to these slights gracefully. That "discretion" I described earlier, that ability to alter responses without altering essential motives, does not in itself provide for personal self-defense, especially when one is attacked by the people one has been trying to assist.

For these reasons and others like them, integrity is not a self-sufficient virtue but best exists in balance with other ethical strengths. As Renaissance thinkers (Shakespeare in particular) were fond of pointing out, sometimes it may even be necessary for integrity to disguise itself as something more socially acceptable — to slum about with the miscellaneous dishonesties of polite and impolite society. When such disguisings occur, however, they consist more of irony and self-containment than of outright pretense.

These difficulties and paradoxes suggest others. Because integrity implies independence, and because it so frequently defines itself in contradistinction to popular opinion, it has come to be associated with individualism. Seeing people of integrity happily on their own, confidently facing the odds, we assume that this individualistic sort of happiness and self-confidence is their goal. Given the premises of this chapter, however, such an assumption is unwarranted. Individual isolation may be a consequence of integrity, but would not be so if integrity had not motives more urgent than social acceptance.

It would be wrong, moreover, to identify popular opinion with communality and integrity with isolation. Popular opinion, which could not survive long if it did not gloss over its own internal contradictions, cannot be considered unified except in a rather superficial sense. Individuals in unconscious disagreement with themselves can never reach a full understanding with others. Psychological wholeness, as here described, offers a better hope of such mutual understanding. Accepting its own human identity, integrity is uniquely in position to understand the humanity of others. Possessors of integrity may be subject to isolation as individuals, but it is through their thought and action that we may best learn what we share.

9 Pain

A most poor man, made tame to fortune's blows,
Who by the art of known and feeling sorrows,
Am pregnant to good pity.

— William Shakespeare, *King Lear*

THE SENSE of undiluted wholeness that seems to be a necessary condition for innovative thinking is also, at one end of the spectrum, a sense of pain. The ability to suffer and even appreciate pain is no less basic to creative vision than the joy of discovery.

To understand its relation to creativity, we must first look briefly at pain as a biological function and a historical influence. Biologically, pain is the classic blessing in disguise, a key element in a neurological warning system whose purpose is survival. Darwinian theory, which once considered pain and the fear of pain to be tokens of a "weaker" nature, has now realized that these conditions are evolutionary strengths, enabling species to avoid or neutralize dangerous challenges. Humanity has developed these strengths far beyond the other animals. Humanity is preeminent not only in the variety of its fears and pains, but in its ability to locate and deal with them. Humanity has cultivated the virtue, unique in nature, of overriding fear and pain, when circumstances seem to warrant it, by a conscious act of will. Human beings thus have the dual evolutionary advantage of feeling pain "better" than other animals and of consciously enduring pain as a means to some desired end.

From this perspective, pain may be seen as an essential element in human progress. As the quotation from *King Lear* suggests, our own pains teach us sympathy; the personal experience of pain provides the matrix by which individuals may feel sympathy for the sufferings of others. Machiavelli argued that politics itself grew out of an awareness of shared suffering. Thus pain has been a key factor in the development of human courage and dignity.

Analogously, pain has functioned as a stimulus to material progress. Fear, pain, and grief helped to provoke the medical advances that have exponentially increased the human presence on earth. More generally, pain in effect has profited humanity, through reverse English, by constituting a natural threat that humanity has set itself up to conquer. If pain is physiologically a defensive warning signal, it is historically a spur to the expansion, through technology, of human power.

As though in emulation of technology, other modern institutions have waged their own offensives against pain. Religious observances, once so full of suffering and awe, have become accommodating and benign. Teachers go out of their way to avoid embarrassing, insulting, overworking, or otherwise vexing their students. Each year public language is further purged of impurities that might injure sensitive groups. Prime-time television series seem dedicated to the comforting message that things are really okay. Indeed, modern society's war on pain has been vastly more successful than its war on pain's causes. By such offensives, modern society has cut one more link between human nature and its dynamic past. The illusory painlessness and fearlessness of our daily lives are an essential part of what it means to be modern.

These developments are supported by a militantly anesthetic

attitude across the board. If readers of this book in the late twentieth century have recently experienced situations provocative of intense pain or terror or grief, it is likely that both they and their colleagues — brothers, sisters, doctors, lawyers, counselors — went all out to mitigate or subdue their feelings, rather than suffering them bravely or appreciating them fully. It is likely, moreover, that free of major pains they are more sensitive to little ones, and that similarly inflationary trends are characteristic of their experience of fear and grief.

With all this in mind, we may wonder whether the modern conquest of pain is a conquest in every sense of the word. In conquering pain we may have suffered a defeat in our battle with ourselves. We may have lost one of the forbidding but strangely gracious environmental circumstances that once gave our character wholeness. And no technical innovation, no feat of bravado, no guarantee of security or power, can make up for the loss of the spirit of the whole.

It is precisely this spirit, conversely, which seems necessary, not only for human evolution in general, but for innovative achievement of any kind. The mind that, whether in the process of analysis or the process of invention, seeks the whole structure with all its implications must also be the mind that is alert to its own full spectrum of potentialities. This spectrum is not limited to those experiences which are pleasant or harmless or uplifting, but necessarily includes their opposites. To be truly open to any experience, the mind must be open to all. The willing endurance of pain is a key factor not only in human dignity, but also in human creativity.

It would seem to follow that individuals who spend their lives in the persistent avoidance of pain are not likely to amount to much. In the first place, they are rejecting the heroic acceptance of suffering that impelled their species to dominance. In the second, they are closing their minds to the wholeness outside of whose context no particular can be considered accurately.

These general aspects of pain and our avoidance of it may be seen as accounting for a number of modern problems that are directly relevant to creativity. I have suggested that effective "discoverers" are characteristically people who have developed professional skills to such a degree that they are wholly internalized and have become second nature. The process of achieving their professional level is usually full of pain. Such mastery demands endless practice of technical operations, endless assaults on seemingly ineluctible concepts, humiliation by teachers, anxious and exhausting competition with peers. To gain such mastery, one must face the sting of pertinent criticism, the shock of a thousand minor failures, and the nagging fear of one's own unimprovable inadequacy.

These pains are seldom eroded by success; as we proceed to higher and higher levels of expertise, and as the stakes get higher and higher, the agonies of excellence reappear in new and frightening ways. A tiny minority gets through to the top, to memorable excellence or profound understanding. The rest of us stop at stages along the way, perhaps for a temporary rest, perhaps for a period of reassessment. But once we stop, we are unlikely to start up again. Security is suddenly far sweeter than enterprise. The sufferings of the ascent, so long endured by insuppressible aspiration, suddenly seem pointless.

What feelings attach to the moment of surrender? Some people feel a lingering regret, a strange sense of lost youth. But those more seriously bitten by the worm of surrender, no matter how early in life it attacks them, grow smug and develop respectable bellies.

One might reply that most people who surrender simply lack the ability to get very far. But it is more accurate to say that ability and intelligence, rightly understood, include a readiness to face pain, while those characteristics which we loosely term "inadequacy" and "ignorance" are typically associated with the avoidance of pain.

Of course avoidance and its consequences bring with them,

almost inevitably, a second pain: the inward or public embarrassment of failure. But especially in modern times, society has found a way of avoiding this pain, too. Modern society has evolved an idiomatic defense of nonachievement so subtle and elegant that it almost makes failure attractive. We can equivocate with failure by saying that we could not stand "the pressure." We can inflate mediocrity by calling cow colleges universities, by naming herds of middle-level executives vice presidents or partners, and by a thousand other sorts of venal hype. We can invert the moral standard by defending a fellow nonachiever as being too sensitive or even too good for the chosen arena. We can espouse a perfectionism so severe that not a single palpable expression can escape its gravitational field, or a philosophy so mystical that it dissolves the whole context of endeavor. We can inveigh, in terms that vary with the times, against the prejudices of the times, and if all these excuses for failure fail, we can blame the system.

This double rejection of pain — a surrender sanctified by a euphemism — has in our time achieved institutional status. Because it includes its own antimorality, it can be passed on with pride from generation to generation. Other ages may have been as full of nonachievers as ours, but no other age, I believe, has developed so comprehensive a rhetoric of failure.

To conclude, then: those people in quest of intellectual dignity and independence in the late twentieth century must act in a cultural context that has done its best to annul or camouflage one of the key elements in this quest, the challenge of pain. For this reason such people currently labor under a double burden: they must face the pains inherent in their task, and they must do so in a culture that has little appreciation for their suffering.

PAIN IN THE CREATIVE PROCESS

Given all this, we might say that the creative process, which is full of pain, constitutes in the modern world a kind of return to nature, a reengagement with the conflict and challenge typical of primitive human experience. The creative process, which has always been painful and hazardous, seems even more so by comparison to the anesthesia of most other modern encounters. No evasions, compromises, or euphemisms soften the pain of solitary innovators. They must face in every project the possibility of total failure; they must take action and accept its consequences.

In addition to the professional agonies outlined, four distinct types of pain may be associated with the creative process: pain of perception, pain of expression, pain of closure, pain of self-suppression. To each of these pains is attached, as though in a fairy tale or moral fable, a special pleasure rewarding the brave sufferer.

PAIN OF PERCEPTION

Like our five physiological senses, which are doorways between the mind and the physical world, our mental faculties operate as doors that may be opened or closed. Our five senses, in ways that spring necessarily from their receptive functions, are doorways both to pleasure and to pain. Our instinct is to avoid physical discomfort whenever it threatens. We shut our ears to the jackhammer and hold our noses driving past the factory.

Analogous prohibitions operate with the mental faculties. We close our minds to many difficulties because of the painful labor involved in confronting them. We abort inquiries that threaten terrible revelations, and beyond what we might learn from outside lies an even more potent threat. Opening the doors of perception is tantamount to opening the doors to our inner selves, exposing beneath protective cloth the nakedness of our own spirits. We fear the power of our own emotions; we fear that our resources, once exposed, will be tried in the balance and found wanting. Creative people can confront and suspend these prohibitions. Like swimmers who learn to open their eyes under water, people of vision deny the impulse of self-protection. In so doing, they turn their vulnerability into a source of excitement and strength.

PAIN OF EXPRESSION

It is draining and depressing to sit motionless before a type-writer or drafting board, or tongue-tied at a committee meeting, or to lie awake in bed turning over and over an idea that always short-circuits at a critical connection. Bad as it is, this pain is often the price we unconsciously pay in fear of what appears to be an even greater evil: the pain of taking an initiative. Surfacing in phenomena like writer's block and stage fright, this is less a fear of the consequences of a projected action than a pure terror of action itself. Hunters call it buck fever: a strange paralysis that confronts us when we face, in its always-sudden wildness, the big moment, the real thing. Unlike consequence-directed fears, those for example of the neophyte swimmer or downhill skier, the fear of self-expression is not fear of failure and therefore does not necessarily vanish after successful action.

The most effective antidote to pain of expression lies in a paradoxical inversion: an understanding that, appearances to the contrary, fear and pain are often positive signals, signs that some great inner prize is at hand. To suffer this way is to be rich in pain, to move in a threatening cloud that can explode into a flash of understanding. Moreover, those who have breached the wall of pain have felt a pleasure in every way equal to it: the pure joy of the act, the exhilaration and wonder that result from the breakthrough into freedom.

PAIN OF CLOSURE

As though the pain of initiating action were not enough, we have inherited as a kind of bonus the pain of *completing* action. Like lovers who can begin but not consummate the act of love, we work vigorously toward the completion of a project but balk at the final step. Manuscripts, complete but for the last revision, rot in filing cabinets; family plans or departmental policies, worked out over hours of discussion, are shelved pending further developments.

This pain, and our fear of it, have several causes. We fear the consequences of the completed act, forgetting that the consequences of inaction are often more terrible and irrevocable. We fear that the finality of a thing done will rob us of freedom, forgetting that real freedom is a process or cycle that consists not only of option but of action. We fear the negative response of our associates, forgetting that this pain pales by comparison with our existing agonies of self-reproach.

All these fears have some validity, but if we give in to them, it is as if we had never thought at all. Closure or presentation is implicit in the fabric of creativity; it is like the eggshell of inspiration, the juncture between the inner energy and the responsive environment. The act of closure is what at last makes a project real to its inventor, infusing in him or her the ancient human pleasure of having built. This satisfaction is uniquely effective in preparing the mind for future projects.

PAIN OF SELF-SUPPRESSION

There is, finally, a pain that may occur at any stage of an independent creative project: the pain of discovering that our work is seriously flawed. Such discovery suggests a choice (itself painful) between two alternatives: we may choose to revise or we may trash the whole project. There is something menacing and nasty about revision, like approaching one's own drywall with a fireman's ax. Behind this distaste, moreover, lurks the chance of a second failure, more shameful than the first. Dumping the whole project seems worse yet. No matter how well justified, the suppression of poor work carries with it bitter shame and a sense of waste; there is something quietly suicidal about destroying the work of one's own hands.

But total readiness to suppress inferior work is one of the keys to effective production. Unless we are willing to throw out our own junk, we lose critical perspective; worse yet, we may gradually lose the boldness to try risky new projects. Scrapping our own failures implies a psychological strength that is essential to successful innovation: it is a declaration of independence, a statement that the innovator, though committed, is ultimately distinct from his or her projects. It also asserts a trust in the future, a confidence in the renewal of one's strength.

I have briefly mentioned the pleasures that await those who can endure the pains described above, and that are as liberating and delightful as these pains are constricting and unpleasant. Like the satisfaction we derive from other tasks, these pleasures partake of willed action, intense involvement, and the satisfaction of completed work. But creative work carries with it other joys that are surely unique. An individual working alone on a plan, a poem, or an experiment feels a total responsibility and control that are lacking in any other field of action. The experience of single-handedly creating something from nothing is also unique, as is the sense that what has been created may be a complete expression of character and assertion of identity. The joys of single insights or happy closures are unlike any other form of pleasure.

Pain and fear of pain, finally, are the necessary conditions for courage. Creative achievement may seem solitary, even peripheral to society, but there is something genuinely heroic about it. Innovative thinkers, as I hope to show in the next chapter, need courage not only in completing their own work but in facing society's response to it. And from an evolutionary perspective, it is they who most fully embody that form of heroism which gives force to the whole human project: the heroism of the seeking mind. It is perhaps this sense of heroism that makes creative endeavor so uniquely enjoyable, that justifies all the pain.

10 *Courage*

Personal knowledge is an intellectual commitment, and as such inherently hazardous.

— Michael Polanyi, *Personal Knowledge*

Man Ray, at age eighty-one, attending a lavish exhibition of his own work in a wheelchair: "If this had only happened forty years ago, I might well have been encouraged."

EVERY PERSON lives in two worlds, one buzzing with the more or less friendly noises of society, the other quietly savage, full of unspecified danger and boundless promise. The first is the social world, in which our security and happiness as individuals depend upon our performing certain functions in certain ways and places, and at certain times. Our given social world, which evolved from a context of infinite possibilities and exists as one of a thousand cultural alternatives, nonetheless asserts itself so comprehensively as to seem the only possible world, shaping our language, legislating our identity.

The second world is the domain of our plastic and dynamic humanity, of those forces within us which are subdued, often arbitrarily and never conclusively, by the rulings of society. It is the world of farce and tragedy, of idyll and outrage. It knows no distinct barriers from the social world but exists in the town of society like a network of obscure alleyways opening up into unfrequented squares, delightful gardens, wild taverns, or the solitude of an empty plain. Though most of our waking lives are spent outside of this world, our occasional glimpses into it, in moments of hilarity or grief or passion, can be unforgettably intense.

Creative people seem more at ease with this dualism than others. They are more open to the inner dimensions of their own characters. They can balance the opposite demands of the tame and the wild, the cooked and the raw, in such a way as to accept the validity of both without admitting the dominance of either. The effort required to sustain this balance, and such other necessary requirements as complete commitment, exhausting practice, prolonged concentration, and the maintenance of an open mind, demands substantial fortitude. It is not the sort of courage we ascribe to great heroes in battle or undaunted revolutionaries. But it is courage nonetheless.

More swashbuckling sorts of courage are likely to be necessary as well. Innovative vision, especially in its more dramatic forms, has an ambiguous effect on an individual's relationship to society at large. On the one hand, innovation is a social act, offering new insight to fellow human beings. Human society, whose sum and substance are based on the achievements of the mind, cherishes and rewards the thinkers to whom it feels indebted. On the other hand, innovation is often an alienating act, not only because of the intensive study and concentration it normally requires, but also because the initial effect of anything new on society always contains an element of shock. We all know well that instant of shocked pause between the utterance of some devastatingly witty comment and the laughter that follows. With more profound innovations this pause is proportionally longer, sometimes long enough to outwear the innovator's life.

In his insightful book *The Courage to Create,* Rollo May expands upon the social dimension of "creative courage":

> Whereas moral courage is the righting of wrongs, creative courage, in contrast, is the discovering of new forms, new symbols, new patterns on which a new society can be built.

Society can respond less than kindly to creative achievement because

> the creative artist and the poet and saint must fight the *actual* (as opposed to the ideal) gods of our society — the god of conformism as well as the gods of apathy, material success and exploitative power. These are the "idols" of our society that are worshiped by multitudes of people.

Let me enlarge on May's point. Society tends to resist innovation for numerous reasons, some quite valid, others less so. To begin, many new ideas do not hold water. They are internally unsound or outlandishly irrelevant or old ideas in disguise or half-baked theories in need of massive development. Many other new ideas, moreover, though sound in and of themselves, are unsound in terms of their implications in the broader context. They are justly rejected as organizationally impractical or overly expensive or potentially disruptive. Society's reluctance to lavish attention on new ideas — its cautious, even suspicious attitude toward innovation — is therefore based on a valid appreciation of the law of averages.

More visceral revulsions operate as well. After all, supporting someone else's new idea means sharing that person's risk. An innovator may ask for our help, speaking eloquently of new benefits and opportunities; but what we hear instead is "Risk your time, money, and reputation for me, following untraveled ways, for some indefinite and perhaps ephemeral reward." Besides, the innovation may threaten our territory. Many valid new ideas endanger the interests vested in established theories, and no professional field, no matter how enthusiastically it endorses innovation, is free from a nagging and purely self-interested resentment of newness.

There is, moreover, the natural dynamics of the generations. The essential power of most institutions resides in people who are between fifty-five and sixty-five years old. Because of their age and the nature of their responsibilities, these people seldom innovate on their own and tend to favor conservative strategies. They are guarded, so to speak, by their would-be heirs apparent, people of forty to fifty-five who compete for succession under the watchful eyes of their elders. The younger people are allowed, even expected, to innovate, but they must do so in such a way as to please their conservative-minded chiefs. In other words, they must innovate genteelly.

Finally, the majority of noninnovators are disinclined to look into the implications of new ideas because, operating in a web of commonly accepted assumptions, they are categorically unaccustomed to looking into the implications of anything at all. Their disinclination becomes something crustier, something more like anger, when a new idea seems to challenge one or more of the assumptions on which their agenda is based.

Beneath these specific difficulties lies a far more general issue, a disjunction that is the by-product of all stable societies. Modern civilization is a vast economic system in which, to be cost-effective, most procedures must be communally adhered to and duplicated over time. Under these circumstances, experimentation must be seen as a restricted specialty, innovation an occasional luxury. The very security we enjoy in society creates a surface tension that can be as resistant to valid new ideas as it is to harmful incursions. This resistance is no more than the shadow cast by a culture's dominant virtues, a sacrifice that must be made so that other goods may endure, a walling over of the secret town so that public affairs can go on more peacefully. Useful as it may be, however, it functions as a curb on innovation and hence as a challenge to innovators' courage.

Does this mean that all or nearly all innovators have to face social resentment? Not at all. Innovators may be lucky enough to land in receptive systems. Innovators may practice what I call the diplomacy of invention and implement new ideas without whipping up disapproval. They may initiate their own schools or companies. They may freelance. But whether they are resented, tolerated, or even idolized, insightful people are not likely to be understood in their own terms. No matter what their real contribution is, they will be praised or condemned according to society's perception of its own short-term needs. If condemned, they will share the cellar with misfits and drudges. If praised, they will find themselves cherished in company with glad-handing contrivers who have passed whole lives without being inconvenienced by a single authentic idea. The insightful may be consoled by the praise of their intellectual peers, but even this can be very slow in coming. In the final analysis, creativity finds no certain joy and justification except in the task itself.

Such solitude is unavoidable. True vision is not merely an alteration of detail but a challenge to whole structures of understanding. As such, it cannot expect an appropriate social response. The same élan or adventurousness that makes creativity necessary to society also makes it, temporarily at least, inaccessible to society's appreciation. Innovation is a lonely art. The leader who looks out to the frontier must face away from the people who follow.

LIBERALISM AND INTOLERANCE

In liberal society this alienation is particularly subtle. In liberal society everything from automotive ads to addresses by university presidents (and this gamut is often narrower than it seems) informs us that our most precious national resources are human talent and the freedom to express it in new projects. The hidden premises, however, unspoken and sometimes not even apparent to the speaker, are that ideas with active applications will be listened to only if they promise to make quick money for those who listen to them, while contemplative ideas will be indulged only if they satisfy the liberal academy. And the liberal academy is "liberal" not in the sense that it is truly open to all sorts of inquiry in all fields, but rather in the sense that it endorses the limited and specific principles of "liberal" ideology.

Liberal culture, in other words, may be less biased than any other practicable culture, but it conceals what biases it has better, and hence more dangerously, than any other as well.

What is the nature of liberal intolerance? This question is of importance here and will be returned to in more detail in the chapters to follow. For now, however, the following introduction should serve:

Like all ideologies, liberalism is a system of assumptions and beliefs anchored by a vocabulary of major normative words. But while the normative vocabularies of most other ideologies (Marxism, for example, or medieval Christianity) are radical and exclusive in tone, liberalism paradoxically operates on a dogma of openness. Key liberal words include "tolerance," "enlightenment," "fairness," "equality," "realism," "excellence," "open-mindedness," "opportunity," "expression," "humanity," and "freedom." But how can "tolerance" condemn? How can "openness" be closed?

The answer to these questions is complex. The secret of liberal intolerance lies in the limited definitions that liberalism ascribes to these and other key words. To the liberal mind, for example, "tolerant" and "open-minded" carry with them a sense of guilt and the spirit of relativism: an anxious unwillingness to make value judgments, particularly ethical or aesthetic, and a resentment for people who do. "Realistic" has connotations including "modern," "scientific," "objective," "pragmatic," "materialist," "data-driven," and "reductivist"; it therefore suggests the exclusion or condemnation of thinkers who are holistic, valuative, idealistic, or critical of science. "Humane" can mean quietistic. "Fairness" and "equality" imply not just concern for the underprivileged but an unwillingness to set any standards but those that can be met by the great mass of humanity. "Excellence" (when applied to people) is limited to expertise in professional specialties. "Freedom" and "expression" connote mere limitlessness, randomness, and whim, and "enlightened" is a term reserved for individuals who use exactly these words in exactly these ways.

Such automatic assumptions suggest exactly who it is that liberals cannot tolerate. The traditional enemies of liberalism — tyrants, oligarchs, imperialists, radicals, conservatives, fundamentalists, and miscellaneous sticks-in-the-mud — form but the outer layer of this category. Far more upsetting to liberals are original thinkers who question one or more of the automatic associations behind the liberal vocabulary.

The liberal response to innovation reflects these idiosyncrasies. Like any other ideology, liberalism accepts as valid "innovation" any fresh-looking elaboration of its own premises and rejects as intolerable any idea that challenges them. But unlike other ideologies, it forbids its adherents to condemn new ideas simply because they are challenging or offensive. Liberal institutions challenged or offended by new ideas must therefore convey their condemnation in ways that do not tarnish their reputation for tolerance. This problem is dealt with by a reversal of the liberal vocabulary into a set of subtly venomous pejoratives. To question the moral position of modern science, for example, is "unrealistic"; to attack overspecialization is "unprofessional"; to challenge moral relativism is "closed-minded"; to find wisdom in ancient insights is "reactionary." And if at all possible, someone adds that the innovator *lacks tolerance.* Very nasty things can thus be said in very nice ways, and liberalism is able to assume an air of openness while maintaining a significant level of bias.

Additional safety is afforded by an air bag of undifferentiated indulgence and a web of casuistry. Innovators are told that "their ideas are fine" because, by implication, "all ideas are fine." Stunned by the impact of nothingness, they are given the limp handshake and steered toward the door. Support for innovators is withheld by pundits who are likely to maintain simultaneously that the innovations proposed are outlandishly strange and that they have already been tried unsuccessfully. Innovative writings are rejected by journal referees who are journal referees precisely because they endorse the old position, and by editors who would lose their jobs if they accepted anything but what was old, or dished up the old stuff as anything but brilliant novelty.

Liberal rejections are doubly harmful: first, because they are truly intolerant, and second, because they falsify their own motives. Being rejected by a liberal institution is like being dealt a sudden low blow by a mother superior. Such reverses are particularly damaging to the young, who are in no position to see through them and consequently tend to take them seriously. The young may complain that liberalism is wishy-washy but have no way of knowing that it is also biased. Inquisitorial authorities, who pronounce anathema upon the new for the acknowledged reason that it is new, are in this regard healthier historical forces than systems that praise innovation openly and suppress it on the sly. Herein lies the special danger of unexamined liberalism. The danger is not that books will be burned or reformers imprisoned. The danger is that society will trick itself out of its own power to evolve.

Equally challenging to courage are society's positive inducements. These incentives are not epically corrupt, like the power for which Faust sold his soul. They are subtler and more insidious, ranging from the accolades exchanged in turn by senior members of a professional society to the immeasurable satisfactions of simply belonging. These latter satisfactions include not only friendship and trust but also a comprehensive protection policy. "Enlightenment" protects us from having to make value judgments, "humanity" from having to take action, "realism" from having to answer questions about our assumptions. For the price of making a few regular genuflections and casting an occasional jeer, initiates are permanently protected from jeers, ostracism, and loneliness. For the price of not asking unsettling questions or submitting unanticipated ideas, initiates may sleep soundly at night and sleepwalk just as securely by day.

Such mechanisms in general suffice to keep the reigning order strong and to remove the irritants that might disturb its sway. When they do not suffice — when through detailed proof or uncanny persistence some outsider forces a new theory into the canon — a different machine is cranked up. The doors fly open, the outcast is gathered in. Systems undergo speedy transfigurations, histories are revised. Arrogated as common property, the new theory suddenly acquires multiple authorship. It is not just true, it is obvious, and we always thought so. Long used to protecting their ideas from condemnation, successful innovators suddenly must learn to protect them from theft.

LIBERALISM, INNOVATION, AND THE IDEA OF EXCELLENCE

I remarked earlier that when liberals conceive of "excellence," they do so in terms of limited specialized skills rather than broad bands of thought or behavior. I should enlarge on this briefly in terms of its implications on innovation in liberal society.

Liberalism as we know it grew up with modern science, technology, and commerce. Elastic yet muscular, liberalism superbly facilitates the activities of these institutions, allowing all of them generous and sometimes uninhibited scope. Individual liberties, a free press, free markets, and free communication between business and research — all liberal staples — made the West the most prosperous area on earth. The complementary relationship between ideology and industry/prosperity accounts in part for the materialist strain in liberalism.

Prosperous modern cultures are all highly specialized, so liberals have every reason to praise and honor the specialists who power the system. They accord the title "excellence" to such narrow skills — not only in science and business but, by analogy, in the humanities, the arts, and athletics — as liberalism has nourished and thrives on.

Given the fascination with "excellence" in special fields, we might expect people to project it into broader ethical norms. An excellent pianist, for example, or (better) an individual achieving excellence in more than one area, might be termed an excellent person. Groups, regional or ethnic, historically characterized by impressive skills and values, might be called excellent. The moral attitudes of individuals, in terms of grace, dignity, benevolence, courage, and generosity, might by projection be termed excellent or lacking excellence. "Excellence" might grow, by natural projection, from a specialized norm to a concept of the good life.

But no such thing occurs. To a liberal, "excellence" is a technical term conveying no ethical value. Or rather, it is a term whose inescapable ethical implications are chronically ignored.

The reasons for this lie at the heart of liberalism. The free institutions and communications that fuel liberal prosperity are themselves connected to a doctrine of radical equality. This connection owes itself to the great influence of the Christian tradition and the Enlightenment in the framing of modern society. It also derives from the inescapable fact that enterprise is "free" to the extent that all individuals are equally free to pursue it. Truly free enterprise would be impossible in a society in which certain individuals or groups were deemed generically better than others.

Just and necessary as it is, however, the doctrine of equality can narrow our purview. In particular, it can annul two moral applications of the word "excellence": that an individual be deemed generically "excellent" in silent contradistinction to other individuals not so deemed, and that individuals conspicuously lacking excellence be dismissed as inferior. The egalitarianism of the liberal, in other words, may be stretched to the extent of applying "excellence" impersonally to discrete achievements, but not so far as to assign it to the full sweep of individual character or the general conduct of life.

This is both good and bad: good because it creates, to an unprecedented degree, a society in which substantial personal liberty is combined with protection of individuals and groups from subjection, exploitation, and slur; bad because it deprives us of examples and models of moral excellence — sometimes even of the sense that such a thing as moral excellence or the good life exists. The emphasis on justice at the expense of moral virtue can bend native vigor and boldness in the direction of mediocrity and caution. It can produce a number of striking ethical paradoxes: liberty without motivation, sensitivity without discrimination, eloquence without conviction, conscience without self-awareness. It can nurture closet elitists who preach equality. It can engender minds that are driven by information and fearful of insight.

These paradoxes help explain not only liberal ethics but liberal psychology. Though they behave materialistically and relativistically, liberals are neither committed materialists nor committed relativists. Rather, their salient characteristic is a lack of commitment to any one goal or set of ideals — a lack occasioned by the strictures of egalitarianism and the pluralism of the free market. Words like "open-mindedness," "tolerance," "realism," and "enlightenment," far from being avowals of real strength, are subtle means of giving dignity to this disaffection, of escaping the generic liberal nightmare, the specter of impotence.

But even if they avoid this nightmare, liberals have troubled dreams. They are tantalized by reason and haunted by ideals. Expensively educated, widely experienced, freely informed, they experience, willy-nilly, incessant collisions with value. Can concepts like symmetry and wholeness pop up in dozens of disparate perspectives without suggesting underlying general models? Can manifest examples of irrationality and injustice fail to have categorical implications about reason and justice? Liberal dreams are visited by dangerous beauties.

Liberal "intolerance," as shown toward innovative projects, derives from these ethical and psychological factors. Since real innovation always either transcends disciplinary boundaries or reshapes the discipline that it addresses, liberals cannot conceive of it in terms of specialized "excellence." Since innovation is a bold assertion requiring unusual degrees of commitment from its supporters, it clashes with liberal disaffection. And "moral" innovations — ideas at all at variance with the encoded pluralism of the liberal mind — arouse not only egalitarian self-righteousness but also a kind of fox-and-grapes resentment, an anger born half of identification and half of fear.

Some readers may object here that I have done their particular professions injustice, that they and their colleagues are generally open-minded, that valid innovation is to them as the bread of life. They may point to the enormous miscellany of radical agenda, new waves, and other apparent innovations that surface in the media every season. Such readers should be reminded that one of the profoundly held (and therefore most questionable) assumptions of Western intellectuals is that they are open-minded. They should reconsider the "innovative" aspects of their culture with an eye toward whether these are real novelties or mere stylish variations on the prevailing ideology. They might also hunt up a few decade-old news weeklies and book reviews (to whose editors and advertisers phony innovation is as snake oil is to snake oil salesmen) and determine roughly how many novelties bruited in their pages proved to make much difference, and how much has really changed from then to now.

Others may object that my criticism of liberalism is an implicit affirmation of some kind of conservatism. The context of my comments ought to discourage such an opinion. Endorsements of creativity and innovation are not characteristically conservative, and in fact my critique of liberalism boils down to the view that liberalism adheres to, yet conceals, a kind of conservatism of its own.

Flaws in the current liberal perspective, moreover, do not mean that liberalism is to be regarded generically as moribund, evil, or otherwise dispensable. Liberalism is an integral element of democratic culture, a habit of mind that can and must endure. But liberalism will endure healthily only if it has occasional refreshment, and this refreshment must include periodic reviews of its own operative assumptions. Such reviews are potentially painful and will necessarily be resisted by some zealots. But they are necessary if liberalism is to remain a flexible and evolving institution.

THE COURAGE OF INDEPENDENT THOUGHT

Though they may seem misanthropic, considerations such as these would appear to follow unavoidably from the phenomenon of innovative thought. Together with other material in Part 2 of this book, they are intended as a sobering balance to the more carefree discussions in Part 1. "The creative mind" — inspiration, discovery, analysis, imagination, and the sense of beauty — is a happy subject, a comedy of mind based on the psychological harmonics of a single thinking individual. "The ethics of creativity" — integrity, pain, courage, self-knowledge, and freedom — is a problematic subject, because creative achievement imposes specific distinctions between the thinking individual and society at large. These are not just distinctions of comparative insight but rather imply the much greater gaps between competence and excellence, between security and exploration, between caution and risk. No culture, however "liberal," can annul these distinctions, which are part of the fabric of social necessity. No culture can make innovation painless or free of danger.

What, then, is the courage of independent thought? Considering the issues raised in the last three chapters, we may say that such a virtue must be triform, addressing the inner self (Integrity), the challenges of work (Pain) and the social dynamics just outlined. We may say further that it is eclectic, facing miscellaneous adversaries, despising illusory dangers and enduring real ones, accepting limited victories and inevitable losses. Can any single quality of character perform all these functions? To Plato and Aristotle, courage was a kind of knowledge, an awareness of what was or was not really worth fearing, predicated on a broader sense of a good that validated the risk. For our own more specific uses, the following may serve: the courage of innovative thought is not a distinct virtue that can be practiced in and of itself. It is rather a by-product, a strength that is the simple consequence of loving our work and knowing why we love it.

11 *Self-knowledge*

Thinking and spoken discourse are the same thing, except
that what we call thinking is, precisely, the inward dialogue
carried on by the mind with itself without spoken sound.

— Plato, *Sophist*

IF PHILOSOPHY has given us anything of firm authority and last-
ing worth, it is the injunction to self-knowledge. Without self-
knowledge, or at least the effort to attain it, we exist merely
as higher animals, blind to our weakness, unguided in our
strength, possessed of temporal power yet subject to the tyranny of instinct and the fictions of pride. For all our physical
energy and mental aggressiveness, we live by chance and survive, in effect, from day to day. Our unique ability to reflect on
the past and the future is useless without the insight that distin-
guishes fact from wish and exposes, beneath variable disguisings, an unchanging self. The ancient Delphic command "Know
thyself" calls us to seek an elusive dignity. It sets out boldly the
standard by which all else is to be known.

Earlier discussions in this book, such as those concerning inspiration, analysis, imagination, and integrity, have shown how
difficult it is to achieve an accurate awareness of anything at all
without also gaining a kind of self-awareness. This seems true

not only because some topics of study (for example, Mystery in Chapter 4) demand an integration of subject with object, but also because the habit of accurate study seems predicated on a psychology "open" to its own inner powers and motives. Now, however, it is time to look at the question of self-knowledge more specifically. If there is indeed an "ethics of creativity," it must include a self-awareness that reviews and balances all other perceptions. If vision is indeed an act of freedom, vision into oneself is that special act which defines and justifies freedom of all other sorts.

Yet the injunction to self-knowledge is a heavy challenge. No exercise of vision is more grimly demanding than that which takes as its prospect our own power to see. Difficult to achieve, self-knowledge would seem to be impossible to transmit, for the reason that, once transmitted, it could no longer be called knowledge of self. Socrates sought it for years, yet never claimed to have achieved it. His student Plato developed the subject in work after work, but not a single dialogue takes up self-knowledge as its special topic. Montaigne's essays, prefaced by the statement "I am myself the subject of this book," treat this topic somewhat more frankly, suggesting the dramatic contradictions inherent in the character of the individual. Moreover, they convey the author's method of introspection to the reader, who may then adapt it to his or her own case. My own treatment of the subject, which shows the influence of these thinkers but is addressed to modern subject matter, is set forth in an imaginary conversation.

Simmons ran into his old friend Marlin at an academic conference in San Francisco. The chance meeting was such a pleasant shock to both that they decided to skip the afternoon sessions and spend the rest of the day walking by the Bay. They left Marlin's rented car near the Marina and strolled west along the beach toward the Golden Gate.

Simmons had not seen Marlin in more than ten years. Fellow

graduate students, and subsequently colleagues in the same history department, they had parted company when Simmons resigned to accept a headship on another campus. Eventually he had become a dean, and now he was interviewing for vice presidencies. Marlin had taken an opposite course, if course it could be called. He had simply continued the work he began. Neither stylish nor famous, he had published philosophical books whose total sales did not far exceed the number of college libraries that ordered them.

To these professional divergences, perhaps, we might attribute the two men's lack of correspondence with each other over the years. But now their old ease of communication was renewed as though without a pause, and they promised to keep in better touch in the future.

As they strolled beside the yards of the Presidio that fine day, Simmons brought up the subject that concerns us here.

SIMMONS: Have you had your midlife crisis yet?

MARLIN: Mine began at birth.

SIMMONS: You seem to have enjoyed it. Mine started out less pleasantly. It began when Martha and I broke up. I floundered for a while and began to wonder what life was all about. I got depressed and almost stopped working. Then I started self-analysis, and now I'm enjoying my midlife crisis, too.

MARLIN: What do you mean by self-analysis?

SIMMONS: I mean a mixture of things. I have psychotherapy every week from a very good man. I go to seminars at a local psychology institute. I have dinner regularly with a group of people who have had similar problems. It's not any one of these so much as the mixture that seems to be helping.

They were passing the windsurfers' beach. Far beyond the surfers and their bright craft a huge gray container ship was coming in under the bridge. In the flattened perspective, it seemed about to collide with an equally big tanker riding light on its way out into the Pacific.

MARLIN: You still haven't told me what you mean by self-analysis.

SIMMONS: But I thought — haven't I just —

MARLIN: Well, if I really didn't give a hang about what we were discussing, I confess I might be satisfied with what you said. But since we meet so seldom and these are such important matters, I ought to ask you for more. I asked you what self-analysis was, and instead of telling me you mentioned a few activities that seem to be connected with it. In doing so, you've brought up some possible attributes of self-analysis, or methods of conducting it, but you haven't begun to define the process itself. Why don't we start again?

SIMMONS: Sure.

MARLIN: What's self-analysis?

Simmons was suddenly reminded of similar cross-examinations in the past. Two contradictory thoughts flitted through his mind at once: one of the almost childlike eagerness with which Marlin pursued these neo-Socratic investigations, another of the relief of not having to undergo them for the past decade. But now there was no choice. It was Simmons, not Marlin, who had brought up the topic.

SIMMONS: Okay. Self-analysis is inquiry into the self.

MARLIN: With what end in mind?

SIMMONS: I suppose, self-knowledge.

MARLIN: And what's self-knowledge?

SIMMONS: You mean, what is it to me?

MARLIN: Sure.

SIMMONS: I'll tell you some of the things I've been finding out. In the first place, I've discovered (and I can tell you it was a real shock) that I had been going around, doing this and that for forty-eight years, without knowing who I really was. I had been very successful, in a grubby sort of way, passing tests and writing articles and chairing committees, but when you subtracted all the piecework and handshaking, there was nobody left in there. That must have been what got Martha so irate at me. But I don't mean exactly "nobody." Somebody was in there, a real live individual, who for forty-eight years had simply been taking it on the chin, knuckling under to the collective superego, submerging deeper and deeper under piles of certificates. Nobody knew this hidden prisoner, not even — especially — I myself. He was down there in the subbasement, probably sniveling and whimpering for help, but no one heard him.

Well, after Martha left me I had the oddest feeling, of wanting to shout out and having no words. It wasn't just sadness I wanted to shout about either, but longing, helplessness, anger, passion, the whole gamut of things that real people feel. All these feelings were in there, trying to kick through the basement walls, and all together they made me a real person, but they weren't real to me yet, and instead of expressing them in a normal way, I choked on them and thought I was going crazy.

That's when I started to see the therapist. He sat me down and made me talk. First I talked about my fears of insanity, but soon I was talking about the pain, and all the other emotions came charging out after that. It wasn't long before I realized two essential things: one, that having emotions and uncertainties and cravings was not only okay but a sign of real health; two, that society — I mean especially the competitive level of society that I had chosen — often rewards individuals for concealing all these feelings — that is, for concealing character itself.

I've learned much more about myself since then. I'm not all the way yet, but I can feel my emotions and accept them. I feel good about the special characteristics that make me an individual. I don't mind demanding what I want when I think I deserve it, or asking for affection when I need it. I know myself, and I'm happy with what I know.

Clearly Marlin was moved by what he had heard. As they neared the old fort and turned up the pedestrian ramp to the Golden Gate Bridge, he asked many questions — about the breakup with Martha, the chances for reconciliation, the health of Simmons's children (who were both in college), the social opportunities at Simmons's campus, the character and methods of the therapist. He also told Simmons something of the state of his own life, which had cruised into middle age with a kind of shocking serenity. By the time all this had changed hands they were pausing midway along the sidewalk of the bridge and could look east toward the distant tower of their old university and west into the Pacific toward the Farallon Islands. They had not spoken for about a minute when Marlin opened up.

MARLIN: Jim, this talk reminds me of many we had long ago. What I admire especially about you is your openness, the way you admit weakness or search for an answer without being embarrassed. It strikes me that no one can ever learn important things or actually grow stronger without this frankness. I hate to say it, though, but you still owe me an explanation.

SIMMONS: What the blazes for?

MARLIN: You still haven't defined self-analysis or self-knowledge. When you tried the first time, you mentioned a few connected activities. When you tried the second time, you described the fruits of your discovery. I'm sure you've won a kind of knowledge. But I'm not yet sure what sort of knowledge it is. We won't know, I'm afraid, until we've discussed self-knowledge in general.

SIMMONS: All right, Ed, have it your way. It's a great day, and I'm ready for anything.

They walked on.

MARLIN: Let's assume, first of all, that you and I have roughly the same idea in mind when we use a word like "knowledge." Otherwise we'd be talking forever. Let's avoid that and target the word "self." What do you mean by "self"?

SIMMONS: Damn!

MARLIN: I thought you were ready for anything.

SIMMONS: But this is silly. "Self" is a much clearer designator even than "analysis" and "knowledge." We all know what self is.

MARLIN: Define it, then.

SIMMONS (after a pause): The trouble is, there's no word for it.

MARLIN: That's the trouble.

SIMMONS: Suppose we say, "The individual one happens to be." That's what I've been discovering through self-analysis: the individual I am.

MARLIN: But this definition causes trouble.

SIMMONS: I haven't noticed that much trouble.

MARLIN: I think that's because what you have discovered about yourself is valid and healthy, as far as it goes. But you see, it only gets you to a certain point. In the first place, when you say "Self equals individual," you are making an error in logic. There is no such thing as an individual, pure and simple. What else do we imply whenever we use the word?

SIMMONS: The set or group into which an individual falls. But —

MARLIN: So we can speak of individual integers or mollusks or houses, because, so to speak, the genus describes the species and the group defines the individual.

SIMMONS: That's true, logically speaking, but when we use the word "individual" about ourselves, all those implications are understood. We can't go around defining words every time we open our mouths.

MARLIN: Specifically, what implications?

SIMMONS: Obviously, that we are individual human beings.

MARLIN: Good! That's what the word "individuals" really has to mean. One more question. Can you "know" the individual without knowing the set, the species without knowing the genus?

SIMMONS: Strictly speaking, you can't.

MARLIN: Then teachers of self-knowledge should teach us, as comprehensively as possible, about humanity, and students of self should seek as ardently to understand the class into which they fall.

SIMMONS: Apparently.

MARLIN: So this is what happened in your recent self-analysis?

SIMMONS: I guess not. The people I worked with didn't have much to say about humanness. They were trying to revive individuality as distinct from and even as opposed to society.

MARLIN: And you were, too?

SIMMONS: Yes.

MARLIN: So "self," as you all meant it, cannot really mean "individual."

SIMMONS: I guess not.

MARLIN: Then I ask you again, what do you mean by "self"?

SIMMONS: Okay, maybe I see what you're getting at. What we really mean, really think, when we say a word may be very different from what the word logically is supposed to mean. Okay, what am I thinking when I say "self"?

MARLIN: Exactly.

SIMMONS: I am thinking, Some quintessential, some absolute me-ness.

MARLIN: Excellent. That seems to be what most of us mean when we use the word "self." It is that me-ness which we look for in psychotherapy, and which we express in self-expression. All these activities, and many similar ones, concern this latent concept, this psychological meaning of "self."

SIMMONS: Well, that's a relief. I thought we'd never stop looking. But now that we've found it, where does it get us?

MARLIN: Into worse trouble. Think about it.

SIMMONS: Do you mean that, because there's this contradiction between logical meaning and latent meaning, the word is suspect? So what else is new? A lot of words don't make sense logically, but if we all know what we're talking about, they work fine, and what's the difference?

MARLIN: Good shot, Jim. You've just blown up the whole history of philosophy. I was afraid it would crumble some day, market pressures being what they are. But look, I'll tell you what.

The two friends had reached the Marin side of the bridge and were on the little road that leads up the west side of the bay. Marlin suggested staying on the road through Fort Baker to Sausalito.

SIMMONS: Another fort?

MARLIN: Well, there are a lot of forts around here, but generally they're sort of peaceful forts. Let's have a beer at the No Name. Hey, *look out!*

Simmons felt his friend pull him to the right as a large body struck his left arm from behind. Bouncing off him and veering toward the center of the road was something unbelievable: a man, monstrously tall and clinically overweight, dressed in a pink and purple clown's suit, out of control on a tiny skateboard. The giant's deflection from orbit took him directly into the path of the next oncoming vehicle, a mauve Jaguar driven at turnpike speed. Grisly carnage was averted when the vehicle darted to the shoulder and gunned past in a cloud of pebbles. Like airliners after a near miss, both individuals disappeared almost instantly along their way, neither looking back. But Marlin had caught enough of a glimpse of the car's driver to recognize the vestments of a clergyman.

"All right," said Simmons, "let's have a beer."

Their walk into Sausalito was spent discussing the cultural history of Marin County.

At the No Name Bar, Simmons and Marlin slouched in captain's chairs, drinking Mexican beer and eating pistachio nuts. Marlin reminded Simmons of their interrupted discussion of the word "self."

MARLIN: It would be a pity not to go on now. We were on the verge of something big.

SIMMONS: How so?

MARLIN: Let's put it this way. You said that the word "self" didn't mean all that it was cracked up to mean, but that if we all knew what we were talking about when we used it, there was no harm done. What you meant, I suppose, is that if the underlying psychology or latent concept is sound, it doesn't matter whether the exterior structure is perfect or not. Take the word "spirit," for example. We can't be ruthlessly specific about what it means, but this vagueness doesn't pose major difficulties. Take the word "table." You can sit on a table or climb on it to reach a light bulb, but that doesn't make it a chair or a footstool. We can endure ambiguities on the surface because the latent concept is secure.

SIMMONS: Very true.

MARLIN: But there's a different order of words, let me suggest. There are words whose logical difficulties betoken problems in their latent concepts. No one in philosophy has named this order of words. Personally, I call them haunted words. They're as though haunted because in and of themselves they carry chronic contradictions, lurking inconsistencies that make effective thinking difficult, hinder communication, and, in effect, muddy whatever waters these words are thrown into. Plato dealt with many such words — "piety," "virtue," "justice," "love," "courage," and others — showing again and again that their conventional use betokened conceptual uncertainty in the speaker and promoted it in the listener. I submit that such words exist today and that "self" is one of them. Can you see why?

At this point Simmons's mind went blank. He looked up at the evening sky, he squeezed an intractable pistachio, he thought of ordering more beer. A mild spasm of pain in his left arm reminded him of his recent adventure on the road. Then an idea, wholly unpremeditated, coiled and sprang. "I think I do see," he said.

"Tell me," said Marlin, straightening up.

SIMMONS: Forgive me if this sounds confused. It all came in a flash. For starters, the original equation, self equals individual, is correct — not just correct, I mean, but inescapable. And so are its logical implications in terms of self-knowledge. If we are, for example, individual human beings, then understanding ourselves is simply impossible without understanding our humanness, finding out what we share with the rest of the set. On the other hand, the flaw in the latent concept or conventional meaning of "self" is that it implies an individual's radical distinctness from the rest of the set. To put it crudely, Western culture is unanimously equating Self with Me. Its not just an error in logic, but an ideological distortion. It's a gestalt that accommodates all sorts of strange bedfellows — romanticism, entrepreneurism, psychoanalysis, civil libertarianism, and all those books and courses about "the individual and society." This latent concept works out well enough in the marketplace — I mean our marketplace — where there has always been enough to go around and a little polite slobbism is never taken amiss. But the concept has problems, and one of the problems is precisely that it has worked so well.

MARLIN: How so?

SIMMONS: Just because it's worked for so long, people take it to be the whole truth. It's infected the language.

MARLIN: Can you tell me another problem?

SIMMONS: Well, here's a big one. When you analyze "self" along the lines of this gestalt, the buck stops at a giant absolute arbitrary Me. I mean, the analysis stops. There's no further to go, no general principles to derive. True, you can make valuable discoveries, same as I have, but they turn out to be discoveries about only one part of the self, the Me part, if you will. The rest of the self, the other parts of identity, get short shrift and are often even dismissed as environmental. But if we studied these parts, too, we might in the end have something like self-knowledge.

MARLIN: But what are these other parts?

SIMMONS: As I've said, an important one is our communal human identity. Discovering who we are as individuals is impossible without discovering what it means to be human. Ethics and politics, for example, would have to be considered subjects in self-analysis.

MARLIN: Wouldn't these paths dead-end, too?

SIMMONS: I think not, because they don't lead to a short-circuiting concept like the Me. They lead back into the heart of life and ideas, maybe even toward a more general truth that connects them all. They run down channels that resemble a living system or feedback loop rather than all pointing toward the same monolithic Me. On top of that, they lead to ways of putting the Me into perspective.

MARLIN: Can you think of other human identities? What about history, our own profession?

SIMMONS: Maybe.

MARLIN: Why not? If human continuity applies in three dimensions, why not in four? If you are going to share identity with everything on earth that's certifiably human, you can't avoid doing so with the past.

SIMMONS: I guess so, though there are a lot of people writing history these days who wouldn't be of much help.

MARLIN: You could say the same thing about ethics and politics, but that's an issue we'd better discuss later. What about the broader perspective?

SIMMONS: What broader perspective?

MARLIN: Our position in nature. Isn't that part of our identity? Aren't we defined by our place in the biological world, the physical world? Has our identity nothing to do with the fact that we live on a tiny island in limitless space, or that as individuals we are colonies of trillions of cells, each with its own self-regulating system, its own power to reproduce, its own business to perform?

SIMMONS: Isn't that stretching it?

MARLIN: Many quite serious thinkers would agree with you, but the theory of compound human identity that we have adopted leaves little doubt that self-knowledge would have to include some inquiry about nature, and hence some serious attention to the topics and methods of natural science. And look at it from another angle. Science has been one of the great factors in human progress, one of the major means of expressing and developing human identity. It's become an extension of the human personality, like Jupiter's thunderbolt or Cupid's bow. Can we really know ourselves without knowing science?

SIMMONS: I suppose not. But what about all the other major fields? Don't they become necessary for analogous reasons? And, if so, what is self-knowledge, the knowledge of everything?

MARLIN: It would seem so, wouldn't it?

SIMMONS: But isn't that absurd?

MARLIN: Only if the study lacks a focus. This reminds me of an idea you have already put very well: that our other, non-Me identities can place the Me in perspective. If you studied all the arts and sciences just for themselves, or just for learning, you would be a megalomaniac, like the lady who walked into Macy's and asked for one of everything. But if you studied all the arts and sciences as they relate to your identity — to your

Me-ness and humanness and livingness, et cetera — your quest would be valid and practicable. You would be seeking your own position in the web of things. You would be trying to determine exactly what does pertain to the Me, and how it pertains, and what on the other hand is shared, and how it is shared. In making such an effort you would be practicing an art that might validly be called philosophy. And to my mind, you would be following the happiest course of study in the world.

SIMMONS: But how would such a study be conducted? What rationale would we use for choosing the relevant areas of a given study and for making connections or distinctions between the insights of one field and another?

MARLIN: You would need a discipline like this.

SIMMONS: Like what?

MARLIN: Like the talk we've just had. You would want a discipline that constantly asked questions about other disciplines and ideas, about popular words, even about itself and its own words. You would need a study whose subject matter was learning itself, a study whose chief function was to evaluate modes of interpretation and understanding. And this superdiscipline, for all its sophistication, would not lord it over the other disciplines, or remain aloof from them. It would hound and pester them, as though it could never have its fill of questioning and dispute.

At dinner Simmons broached the subject of transportation back to the city. Marlin remembered that the ferryboat could take them from Sausalito back to within a short hop of the car.

On the dock the two friends passed an unmistakable figure: the giant skateboarder. Dressed this time in a tuxedo, he stood under the stars with a violin, playing Tartini. A sizable audience, whose numbers seemed to include every walk of life and style of attire, listened in enchantment.

In the clear evening the ferry ride back to San Francisco was delightful. Simmons reminded Marlin that it had been on such a ride that Van Weyden, the narrator of Jack London's *The Sea Wolf*, had unexpectedly begun the first leg of a voyage that would take him all over the North Pacific. "I also have the sense of having traveled far," he said, "thanks to our walk and our conversation."

MARLIN: You mean, in spite of my mistakes?

SIMMONS: Mistakes? But what you said seemed perfectly sensible.

MARLIN: But what about what I neglected to say? Since we left the No Name, two of my omissions in particular have been bothering me, and it isn't just that I failed to bring up these subjects, but that even if I did, I would not have known quite where to fit them in. I'm convinced that both of them bear on the problem of self-knowledge, but neither of them came to me from the study of philosophy. I learned of them from the poets, especially Sophocles and Shakespeare.

SIMMONS: What were these great omissions?

MARLIN: They're both aspects of self-knowledge that might be seen as balancing the others I have mentioned. The first is a sense of our weakness: our physical and mental limitations, our varying emotions, our brief stay in time. If we learn everything else, but do not learn our own inescapable shortcomings, we will really know very little about ourselves.

SIMMONS: But wouldn't that kind of awareness follow from all the other studies?

MARLIN: It well might, except for the fact that specific studies of the sort I mentioned earlier tend to inebriate rather than to chasten. It is such fun to learn, and learning a little we feel we know so much, that the sense of limitation I describe must come from a source other than straight learning, a source like poetry. Tragedy is a good teacher along these lines; far better is real experience, the personal crisis and suffering that tragedy imitates.

SIMMONS: Well taken. What's your other omission?

MARLIN: It's that, when all is said and done, self-knowledge seems to imply a kind of forgiveness. If what we have said about human continuity is valid, people with self-knowledge are not apt to be self-righteous about the failings of others. Self-knowers may fight for their standards with tooth and nail, but they won't do it sanctimoniously. And these must be people who can also forgive themselves. For what would it be to forgive others and condemn oneself? Like the forgivingness I just mentioned, humility is a quality which, if it can be learned at all, is not approached "through channels," I mean, through the types of objective study we have recommended. We must find these and other very necessary qualities, like courage and integrity, somewhere else. And to say this is to admit that knowledge is not a wholly objective thing and that, I fear, you and I have not discussed the whole of self-knowledge.

SIMMONS: There's always the future.

The ferry pulled up to the bright and crowded city dock. It was late by now, and the two friends caught a cab back to the Marina. Before they parted for the night, Simmons had time for one more question.

SIMMONS: Only one thing bothered me. When I described my own state of mind after therapy, I mentioned having discovered that society compels people to suppress their individuality in order to gain success. But later, our conversation seemed to prove the opposite: that our society was based on individualism. In which case was I wrong?

MARLIN: In neither case, I think. It's just that the loose terminology of self allows for these apparent contradictions. When you lost "individuality" in search of success, you were in fact losing human identity, humanity. Because you were starved for humanity, you were deprived of dignity and thus of a real sense of self. And when we say that Western ideology is based on individualism, we really mean that it is a variety of thought systems whose common denominator is the Me, which does not respect the individual, as we have defined that word, at all. And there's a great paradox here. Not to give you nightmares, Jim, but suppose we tried surgically to isolate the Me, like some anatomical organ, and that we cut away all the other identities, human, natural, cultural, in order to do it. What would we have left?

SIMMONS: I don't think I want to know.

MARLIN (laughing): I won't be *that* specific, except with regard to one thing. I think we would find that the Me in one person is extremely similar to the Me in another. After all, what is the Me but a conscious sense of distinctness? Can't we say on this level that one conscious sense of distinctness is very like another? Doesn't this justify your own feeling that the battle for success in the modern world is fought by nonentities? And paradoxically, doesn't this mean that the ethic of Me is at root a nonindividual ethic, while the idea of compound identity holds the only hope of real individuality?

SIMMONS: That seems to make sense.

MARLIN: So that in fact the only thing that is truly our own is what we truly share.

SIMMONS: So it would appear.

12 Freedom

Liberty is the right of doing whatever the law permits.

— Montesquieu, *The Spirit of the Laws*

They would be subject to no one, neither to lawful ruler nor to the reign of law, but would be altogether and absolutely free. That is the way they got their tyrants, for either servitude or freedom, when it goes to extremes, is an utter bane, while either in due measure is altogether a boon.

— Plato, Eighth Letter

EARLIER I quoted Viktor Frankl's story about the woman whose waning life was transformed by the poetic image of a single tree. That story, to which I suggest the reader return, speaks strikingly of the links between creativity and freedom. Specifically, the woman's ability to identify creatively with the tree as a symbol of "eternal life" freed her from her failing body and her miserable fate. More generally, the story suggests the premise of this chapter: that the creative act is the classic act of freedom and by extension the ultimate justification of the argument for free will.

But this premise demands some preparation. To begin, what

excuse is there for reassessing the most famous word in modern history — the word which, more than any other, is used to name the Western condition? Can there be any doubt about the nature of freedom when it is written into laws and referred to in every tract, letter, and article that even remotely concerns political affairs? Everyone knows what it means to be free, particularly those in countries in which the simplest liberties have been denied. Freedom is, in the words of Montesquieu, "the right of doing whatever the law permits."

This word-of-mouth consensus, however, has little support from serious inquiry. Philosophically, freedom seems to be a topic of deep secrecy. Though the term crops up in most broadly philosophical works, there has not been a major book on freedom since Henri Bergson or Benedetto Croce — some would say since John Stuart Mill. In our free society, with all its freedom of thought, we look in vain for a single regular university course, whether in history, philosophy, political science, or literature, that addresses itself to the analysis of liberty.

Why is the study of freedom avoided? There are two types of subjects that a culture studies little: those which it despises and those which it holds dearest. Freedom is a subject dear to modern Western society, so dear, apparently, that it is habitually quarantined from analysis. We do not examine the concept because it is part of what we assume ourselves to be. The concept of liberty is so embedded in our self-image that, in order to define it truly, we would have to accept the formidable challenge of defining ourselves.

This challenge is also dangerous. Serious analysis would question the word-of-mouth definition of freedom — as a means of establishing this definition more firmly or perhaps improving on it. But to question such a loaded concept, as we have seen in the chapter Courage, is not politically correct. When the famous exile from tyranny, Aleksandr Solzhenitsyn, addressed the topic in a Harvard speech, he did not, as his listeners might have expected, praise the United States as a haven of liberty but rather excoriated it as a "legalistic" society in which too many citizens strive to be as bad as the law allows. He called into question not only American behavior but the philosophical justification for that behavior in Montesquieu. For his pains Solzhenitsyn was sentenced to the liberal equivalent of exile: he was ignored.

Solzhenitsyn was right, of course. But he was right in an incomplete, arbitrary, almost priestly way that made him sound wrong. He ignored a factual irony worthy of great novels: that only a nation whose liberties allowed for selfish excess could have become strong enough to give sanctuary to him and millions of others. A great democratic nation is like a creative mind: its quest for form makes it conversant with monstrosities. In practice, it seems, the temple of political liberty can be approached only by strolling first through the stands of a market and the tents of a carnival.

But this walk is getting rather too long for comfort. As I write at the end of the 1980s, American liberties are straining under what may be their supreme test. Political freedom is exploited by sociopaths who advocate genocidal projects, religious freedom by circus saints whose followers live in stalls. Constitutional guarantees are stretched by well-meaning judges and well-paid lawyers to a reach so formidable as to obliterate the meaning of the words "justice" and "crime." An epidemic of irresponsible takeovers has lessened economic diversity, shattered corporate stability, and, through junk bonds, weakened the fabric of American investment. Lobbies manipulate both Constitution and Congress, and perhaps more than ever before, Congress itself has become a convention of regional lobbyists functioning at the expense of the national interest. Cries of foul play are rebutted with the simple statement that no rules are being broken. The trouble is that the original "rules," as formulated in the eighteenth century, were predicated on assumptions about human reason and moderation that are no longer justifiable.

These manipulations of political liberty are paralleled internationally by an equally unprincipled exploitation of the environment. Government efforts to limit pollution and waste (and even here only the most visibly hideous cases are being addressed) ignore a far greater threat: that a world population growing by a billion every decade, and increasingly demanding of technological conveniences, will make short work of existing energy sources and tear the environment to shreds. In the final analysis, this global orgy of consumption closely resembles the self-interested legalism we Americans see at home. In both cases legal freedoms are abused by individuals and groups who see in available liberty an opportunity for rapacious excess. In both cases long-term communal interests are dismissed in favor of short-term subjective gratifications.

The question that concerns me is not whether or how this abused freedom is to be restrained; it is, more basically, whether it is really "freedom" at all. In order to answer this question, let me offer two general models of liberty that will support or illuminate more specific applications. Models of this sort are usually sought in psychology or ethics. Mine come from nature.

Physics and biology suggest two distinct ideas of freedom. In physics, the freedom of a given object is inversely proportional to the influence of extrinsic forces upon it. A ball bearing in a deployed satellite is freer from planetary gravity than it would be on the surface of the earth. A rock in free fall is unimpeded in its descent. Water molecules in the liquid or gaseous state are freer than they are in the frozen state. Thus physical freedom is a negative quality, implying lack of compulsion, inhibition, or limit. As such, it is no less amenable to mechanistic analysis than the forces that work around it.

Biological freedom is a radically different concept. Viewed across evolutionary history, life is a free form — free in its unique capacity to respond to extrinsic forces, exploit them, and, at its most complex level, understand and control them. Evolving life is morphogenetic, "form breeding"; evolving life is like a kaleidoscopic succession of art forms. Biological freedom is thus a positive quality and one that defies mechanistic analysis. Had some interplanetary intelligence, before the start of life on earth, known everything there was to know about pre–living matter, it would have been unable to predict earthly life in its current state. The physical and biological models of freedom have parallels in the human sphere. Physical freedom, as negative freedom from extrinsic force, is analogous to Montesquieu's concept of liberty as "the right of doing whatever the law permits." Law, as extrinsic force, generates directives and prohibitions that citizens must honor. But where law is silent, the will has free play.

Can the dynamics of this political freedom, like the dynamics of physical freedom, be analyzed mechanistically? Certainly not in individual cases. But political science, as practiced since Socrates, is based on the idea that given a specific set of historical, political, and economic circumstances, the responses of populations are predictable.

We can appreciate such predictability without becoming political scientists. The national and global exploitation of liberties is a classic example of it. This exploitation illustrates a "law" or universal prediction about history that was implicit in the classics and later codified by Machiavelli and Hobbes: that any society which is not galvanized by national emergency, tempered by wise laws, or inwardly sustained by religious or moral value will degenerate into an anarchy of self-seeking. In such a material- and power-driven society, the idea of "freedom" as uninhibited personal choice ceases to apply: individuals move in mechanistic and predictable courses to protect or enlarge their interests.

Paradoxically, then, political freedom can call forth its own opposite: unduly stretched, it can be a mandate for mechanistic behavior. And mechanistic behavior, rather than any real expression of freedom, is presently threatening democratic institutions and the world at large.

Human creativity presents a stronger model of freedom. Analogous to what I called biological freedom, creativity may also be seen as the ultimate extension of that liberty: the preeminent evolutionary sophistication. Like evolving nature, human creativity is morphogenetic. Because it breeds new forms, and because these new forms necessitate reactions from the human and nonhuman response systems around them, creativity drives an evolving external context, remakes its world.

This morphogenetic capacity makes creativity a more dependable basis for a theory of freedom than the prevailing model, rational choice. Rational choice theory conceives of an individual choosing freely among a number of specific alternatives. The creative mind, on the other hand, does not conceive of the will, or of reality in general, in terms of limited alternatives. Creativity can recontextualize experience, producing new alternatives and opportunities. Rational choice means limited options in a fixed world; creative choice rebuilds the world, constituting a potentially infinite fund of future options.

Examples of this phenomenon abound. Perhaps the most effective are those which readers may find in memories of their own experience. But I will give a few, if only to provide a context.

In *Innovation and Entrepreneurship*, Peter F. Drucker writes of a crisis in the history of the ocean-going freighter.

> In the early 1950s, the ocean-going freighter was believed to be dying. The general forecast was that it would be replaced by air freight, except for bulk commodities. Costs of ocean freight were rising at a fast clip, and it took longer and longer to get merchandise delivered by freighter as one port after another became badly congested. . . .

The basic reason was that the shipping industry had misdirected its efforts toward nonresults for many years. It had tried to design and build faster ships, and ships that required less fuel and a smaller crew. It concentrated on the economics of the ship while at sea and in transit from one port to another.

But a ship is capital equipment, and for all capital equipment the biggest cost is the cost of not working, during which interest has to be paid while the equipment does not earn. Everybody in the industry knew, of course, that the main expense of a ship is interest on the investment. Yet the industry kept on concentrating its efforts on costs that are already quite low — the costs of the ship while at sea and doing work.

The solution was simple: uncouple loading from stowing. Do the loading on land, where there is ample space and where it can be performed before the ship is in port. Concentrate, in other words, on the costs of not working rather than on those of working. The answer was the roll-on, roll-off ship and the container ship.

To call this an example of elegant problem solving is to miss the point. The problem as originally conceived (How to make the hauling of freight over oceans cheap enough to be profitable) was never "solved." Instead, a new problem (How to cut losses on ocean-going freighters qua capital investments) was substituted. The new problem had the virtue of describing reality more comprehensively and accurately than the old. It generated new alternatives, which led in turn to innovation and profit.

The redefinition of problems is a creative act that has interesting implications in professional and personal life. It involves an aggressive rebuilding of reality and is, by implication, a declaration of personal freedom. It is based on the seemingly absurd but often viable premise that if one feels uncomfortable with a major problem in life, one may simply trash it, saying something like, "I don't like this problem. I want a bigger, bolder problem, or a fatter, happier one."

In some cases creative redefinition is so radical as to constitute a kind of paradox. Reality may so greatly diverge from our mental conception of it as to be nearly opposite, or quite opposite, to what we believe. Strategies opposite to perceived reality or common sense may succeed, and in succeeding open up new images of reality.

Sport, which is as rich a field for creative freedom as any, offers an example of paradoxical strategy called "playing their strength." This applies in tennis, in which if your opponent has a strong forehand, you may play to it, working the opponent over toward the forehand side and opening the backhand side for a strong approach shot. It applies in football, in which an offensive player runs right at a defensive end who is known to be the quickest man on the line (thus neutralizing his quickness). Both strategies involve a redefinition of experience in which a power to be feared is reconceived as an opportunity to be mined.

A similarly paradoxical strategy worked on an American college campus in the 1960s. Under heavy siege from students on a broad spectrum of issues, the university administration felt particularly pressured by the brilliant antiestablishment polemics of a young humanities professor. Having determined that neither diplomacy nor authority could dissuade this fiery pedant from his (to them) misguided opinions, the administration took the unlikely step of elevating him to the position of associate dean for student affairs. This job put him at the nerve center of all information relevant to student unrest, gave him a voice in administration strategy planning vis-à-vis the students, and endowed him with substantial power and responsibility in evaluating individual cases.

This apparent blunder was actually a work of wisdom. Of course the brilliant polemics ceased immediately. The dean's office soon became, at least in the opinion of students, a place they could better trust. And the young professor, in his administrative actions and professional publications, grew in both moderation and maturity.

On a far more massive scale was the paradoxical reconstitution of reality achieved by the early Christians. Here the ethical context of imperial Rome, an ideology rooted in military, political, and economic power, was rejected in favor of its opposite, an ethic of humility and otherworldliness. This epochal innovation was in part the work of Saint Paul, whose oratorical letters paradoxically reworked the language of Roman power into a metaphor for Christian spirituality.

> Therefore, take up God's armour; then you will be able to stand your ground when things are at their worst . . . Stand firm, I say. Fasten on the belt of truth; for coat of mail put on integrity; let the shoes on your feet be the gospel of peace, to give you firm footing; and, with all these, take up the great shield of faith, with which you will be able to quench all the flaming arrows of the evil one.

Such innovative eloquence not only won many converts away from the Roman cause but stole some Roman thunder in the process.

Saint Paul's example suggests, finally, creative redefinitions that are inspired or poetic. Viktor Frankl's patient who found a life-redeeming metaphor in a single tree prospered through such an act. By identifying with the tree as "eternal life," she turned her own life into a work of art — one which, for all we know, touched a reality deeper than the material reality of her death. We might say more generally that every great work of art is an act of creative liberty because it enhances human self-knowledge. But this type of liberation can operate in the sciences as well. William Harvey's heart/pump metaphor was basically poetic. Pumps are human artifacts; hearts are not. But Harvey's metaphor made the human body accessible to mind and medicine in a revolutionary way.

These examples demonstrate the power of creative liberty and suggest its immense scope in human affairs. They present the possibility that, rightly nurtured, creative freedom can generate new contexts and alternatives that will renew the political sphere. Less tangible, less legally controllable than political freedom, creative freedom is nonetheless what justifies legal freedom and what can uniquely preserve it. Political liberty is a finite resource; after a certain point, one cannot increase one's own share of it without a concomitant decrease in the freedom of others. Creative freedom knows no such quasi-physical limitations, but builds new theaters for its own exercise. And creative freedom grows, rather than contracts, when it is shared.

Thus it lies with democratic governments and individuals not only to maintain reasonable and nonerosive levels of legal liberty but, more dramatically, to foster and renew creative freedom. This mandate applies, morever, not only to advanced professional disciplines but also to the education of the young.

PART III

*The
Politics
of
Innovation*

13 *Introduction*

THE FIRST of the following two stories is rather surprising, the second almost unbelievable.

Ludwig van Beethoven originally completed his Quartet No. 13 in B-flat, Op. 130, with the long piece of highly innovative music that we now know as the Great Fugue (*Grosse Fuge*). In its original form, the work was certainly the longest and probably the most monumentally daring of all his quartets: a subtly developed set of six movements culminating in an electrically powerful fugue. Initial response to the quartet was troubled: the fugue taxed the strength of both audience and musicians. Beethoven was moved by these early responses and undertook to write something more pleasing. The short allegro with which he replaced the Great Fugue was probably the last piece of music he ever completed.

Though the Great Fugue was performed as an individual concert piece for decades, the Quartet was not played in its original form until this century.

During the second and third decades of the seventeenth century a figure much talked about in London and on the Continent was the Dutch inventor Cornelis Drebbel. A strong, good-looking man who always spoke gently and never wore a sword,

Drebbel was nonetheless a lion of technological innovation. His perpetual-motion machines fascinated the two most intellectual monarchs in Europe, James I of England and Emperor Rudolph II of Prague. Drebbel was famed as a designer of microscopes and telescopes. Other inventions that brought him international renown included a "magic lantern" for producing visual illusions, new methods for refrigeration and incubation, self-playing musical instruments, and a highly effective scarlet dye. Drebbel's innovative capabilities were attested to by figures as notable as Bacon, Galileo, Rubens, Huygens, and Leibniz.

Three of Drebbel's projects were especially remarkable.

In 1620 Drebbel designed, produced, and tested the world's first working submarine, a vessel capable of holding twelve sailors who could propel it under water with oars. This underwater navigation was possible for indefinite periods of time, because Drebbel had isolated, bottled, and shipped aboard pure oxygen for his sailors to breathe.

Some years later Drebbel produced self-propelled explosive marine armaments that were employed against enemy ships by the British in the second La Rochelle expedition.

In 1623 or 1624 Drebbel approached the Prince of Wales with an unusual plan that would cost, Drebbel thought, about £20,000. Drebbel wished to build, on a little hill near the city limits, a massive solar device that would, via conduits, heat all of London. The design of this device, numerous mirrors focusing on a heat accumulator, was generally similar to large solar heating projects not put in place until the late twentieth century (even Drebbel's English biographer, a historian of engineering working in the late 1950s, thought this project "fanciful").

None of these schemes gained Drebbel success or fortune. The submarine, successfully tested in the Thames, became a mere conversation piece and proceeded to rot at anchor. The torpedoes failed in battle (apparently because they were not deployed close enough to the enemy) and brought Drebbel nothing but bitter embarrassment. The solar heating plan was rejected. Drebbel spent his declining years as proprietor of a riverside pub. In succeeding centuries his name fell into near oblivion. The eleventh edition of the *Encyclopaedia Britannica* (1910–11) mentions him briefly, as two different men.

I bring up these stories as examples of the profound effect that social response can have on the quality of creative achievement, not only as an influence on the innovators themselves, but as a means of defining innovative production over history.

Beethoven wrote his B-flat Quartet at the height of his career. He was known all over Europe, courted by aristocracy, revered almost religiously as a bold innovator by younger composers like Schubert. He was serenely confident in the value of his achievement. Why should he decapitate one of his most daring works in deference to the results of a first hearing? Of all possible answers, the one most likely is that, like all artists, from epic poets to village fiddlers, he wished to please, and that no quantity of acclaim could rid him of this wish.

Drebbel, who was a technological innovator on a par with Edison, never gained financial security. Famed in his own time, he became one of technology's forgotten men. How can history have produced this combination of triumph and flop? Again, one answer seems likelier than any other: society had no conscious need for what Drebbel produced, brilliant innovations though they were; and history forgot Drebbel because society has no mechanism for remembering things it does not need. Drebbel ended up dispensing a product whose importance to society was unquestionable: beer.

Clearly the relation between creative achievement and audience is not one way. Most creative people not only aim their projects toward social acceptance but modify them according to society's real or imagined reaction. Even innovators like

Beethoven can feel solidarity with their social environment so deeply as to alter their creations in response to social feedback. Innovators who lack this sociohistorical sensibility walk a perilous trail. They are misunderstood or ignored in their lifetime, and more ominous yet, are written out of history. Our historical model of innovation is not a model of all great ideas but a model of the great ideas we used.

Even our historical picture of successful ideas is somewhat clouded. When we look at triumphant innovations of the past, we see them, so to speak, from their own future: we confront them as *faits accomplis,* hardened into the sedate structure of our own cultural background. Heliocentricity, liberal democracy, the circulation of blood: it takes a major feat of imagination to recapture the drama of these ideas in the making. It takes uncommon open-mindedness to understand how, as stable citizens at the time of their introduction, we might have reacted to them ourselves.

Our blindness to these subjects, coupled with our historical neglect of valid innovations that failed, helps build the illusion, common in liberal society, that innovation is easy, that, as Bernard Lonergan ironically puts it, progress is automatic. Our blindness also makes us insensitive to the dramatic forces, plastic and inchoate, that are the roots of our future.

Of all the hidden conditions pertaining to the interplay of creativity and society, perhaps the most universal is conflict: a political surface tension broken by the creative act, a reluctance (momentary or extended) in the social response, and a resultant bitterness in the mind of the creator. Drebbel and Beethoven were by no means the first to experience this conflict; indeed, it is imprinted in our mythic history. Adam and Eve ate of the fruit of knowledge and earned the wrath of God, who declared that Adam had "become as one of us" (Genesis 3:22) — in other words, humanity had gained too much power. Noah's descendants were "of one language" and sought to build on the plain of Shinar a tower "whose top may reach unto heaven." God put them down, fearing lest otherwise "nothing will be restrained from them, which they have imagined to do" (Genesis 11:1–6). Tiresias was blinded for his wisdom, Icarus shot down for his technological bravado. Oedipus sought new knowledge and won it with a burden of shame. In one sense, these myths imply that innovation is offensive to the godhead because it increases human dominion. In a deeper sense it implies, in humanity itself, a latent neophobia, a fear of change.

The reasons for this resistance and drama derive both from rooted emotion and from common sense. New knowledge is new power, and there is nothing more viscerally shocking than power newborn. The shock of innovation may soften into delight, but it may also turn to fear. After all, the new power offered may be a trick or an illusion. If the power is real, innovators may wish to use it selfishly. The power may challenge established order, in an institution or society at large; it may rock the stable values of peaceful citizens. Innovation is ipso facto dangerous, for if it endangers nothing else, it endangers the safety of a satisfied mind. Society greets the innovator with curiosity and distrust, as the native Americans greeted the Spaniards in armor.

The chapters that follow focus on the drama of innovation in modern liberal society. As I have tried to show in the chapters Courage and Freedom, this drama, though by no means bloody, is often surprisingly grim. Though probably friendlier to innovation than any other form of society, liberal democracy is subject to its own prejudices, blind spots, and other foibles. Among these are a materialism prettied o'er with phrases like "pursuit of happiness," a relativism graced with titles like "open-mindedness," a remarkable distaste for planning, a deep distrust of heroism, and neither last nor least, an intolerance for any ideas that challenge liberal assumptions. In liberal societies the negative response to innovative thinking is characteristically implicit — buried in reticence or disguised by rationalization. In these implicit forms it exerts a more powerful negative force than it possibly could if expressed openly. Innovators, who inevitably must encounter both sheep and wolves, face particularly sharp challenges in a society in which almost everyone looks like a sheep.

For this reason and others, the relation between creativity and its audience is political as well as ethical. Extending into society's self-image and its views about government, science, art, and education, this drama can be approached only through an analysis of such views and the rooted ideological assumptions that support them. The chapters of Part 3 suggest a variety of ways of dealing with such assumptions. The five chapters on education and the arts and sciences (14–18) reflect on the state of innovative thought in those institutions in which we might most expect to find it in power, and speculate on ways in which its power may be increased. The concluding chapters (19–22) expand more broadly on creativity as a political phenomenon and a function of historical change. Just as the first chapters of this study dealt with the beginnings or wellsprings of vision, these final chapters consider its impact on society.

In this last section it will no longer be of much use to lump all innovative and creative thought together and emphasize its common principles. The many branches of innovation in the arts and sciences, in technology and politics, have historically developed strengths and limitations of their own. In some cases the limits of a particular innovative form are generic and permanent; in others they are periodic and capable of repair.

Of particular interest in this regard will be distinctions between innovation in the empirical and nonempirical disciplines. In the natural sciences and in technology, innovative progress is more or less continuous but makes little or no contribution to what might be called humane enlightenment. In the arts and humanities, we note cycle and variation rather than steady development; but conversely, these disciplines are depended on for essential contributions in humane enlightenment. This accounts for the potentially tragic fact that increments to human material power are not paced by increments in the wisdom to use that power, that we are driving faster without necessarily learning to steer better.

Similar distinctions operate in the ways in which scientific and humanistic innovation are resisted by society. Scientific inquiry must break the surface tension of acquired assumptions and vested interests; it must struggle against such mechanisms of reaction as the greed for quick profit, the fear of paradox, the compulsion for closure, and the love of closed systems. But because of the reproducibility of results and an excellent communication system (scientific journals and conferences), most valid ideas ultimately find their way to the world at large.

Humanistic innovation faces heavier odds. It must compete not only with vested interests but with cheap imitations of itself, bred of cynicism or illusion and dolled up in the smock of newness. It must endure the disrespect of scientists who confuse unquantifiabilty with frivolity and the neglect of administrators who think self-knowledge an expendable luxury. It must do all this under the conviction that the domain of reason and insight is not restricted to the material world and that there are forms of valid discovery which have nothing at all to do with incremental progress.

But such odds, while heavy, are far from overwhelming. The immense miscellany of contemporary ideas, together with the treasury of the past, offers a variety of opportunities by which interdisciplinary innovation can combine some of the better aspects of empirical and nonempirical thought. To emphasize these possibilities, the chapters that follow not only discuss innovation but suggest forms of it.

14 On Teaching

The sense of wonder is the mark of the philosopher.

—Plato, *Theaetetus*

DEEP ANTIQUITY accorded its teachers — Chiron, Phoinix, Palamedes, Thoth, Dionysus, Prometheus — the status of heroes or gods. Such veneration, strange to us today, shows a profound awareness of the historical significance of teaching. True teachers, whose daily actions may not seem heroic, are nonetheless the source of what makes humanity itself a sort of hero: they awaken the awareness that makes us preeminent on earth; they store and pass on that knowledge of nature whose incremental growth has vastly enlarged our power. In this evolutionary context, teaching is the characteristic human function, the classic human activity. For this reason, if for no other, the true teacher, no matter what his or her specific field, always instructs us in humanity.

What does it mean, truly to teach? What can be added to the countless books and education school courses that instruct us in the art of teaching? With apologies to those who may feel offended, I add simply that most of these books and courses seem to depend on a false premise. On the face of things, there is no art of teaching. Teaching is, rather, an aspect of all arts; as a division of each art, it cannot be considered an art itself. Arts, we assume, can be taught, but to teach teaching is as absurd as to play playing or to eat eating; in this sense there is no phrase more self-evidently preposterous than the title School of Education.

Arts, moreover, have their rules. One does not play the piano with one's elbows or paint with the brush handle. Teaching would seem to have no such rules; rather, it seems to take what rules it has from the sovereign necessities of its particular subject. You might say that if art imitates nature, teaching imitates art. Different subjects, different necessities, may arbitrate wholly contrary yet mutually effective pedagogical methods. Teaching, it appears, is not a separable entity but part of a continuum that alone gives it meaning.

To accept this premise is to entertain a radical corollary: that every teacher must be, in the truest sense of the word, a scholar or artist. By this I mean one who loves and studies a subject and seeks continually to improve in it. The proper method of teaching a given art is available only to those who, by personally engaging in that art, have become conversant with its inner necessities. The fundamental motive of true teaching is the love that seeks and studies and performs. True teachers not only impart knowledge and method but awaken the love of learning by virtue of their own reflected love.

In modern education at all levels an opposite view obtains. Specialized society has termed teaching itself a specialty, a discrete function cut off equally from its profound sources and its proper goals. Primary and secondary school teachers qualify for their positions by taking courses in "teaching" and, once qualified, devote their careers exclusively to classroom activities. The professional establishment may encourage them now and then to improve their "teaching skills" but does not allow them time for the active pursuit of the particular art they teach. Instead of being required or even allowed to improve their understanding or increase their creativity, they are largely condemned to repetitive activities, routine tasks whose dynamics belies the beauty and grandeur of the subjects they address.

As though aware of this exploitation and demeanment, society accords these teachers a relatively low level of respect and a minimum of financial security. The teacher, once a hero of society, is presently its drudge.

Higher education seems to offer a brighter picture. Would-be college professors generally do not take courses in "teaching." Mastery of the fundamentals of teaching is, in the main, assumed to be a by-product of proper graduate education. On many campuses, moreover, the necessity for professors to publish assures some form of active contact between teachers and their art. But these advantages are counterbalanced by the following weaknesses:

First, most scholars cannot publish except in highly specialized areas. The "art" they practice is not a total art but a fragmentary or tangential pursuit. Although it is assumed that university professors remain in touch with the general principles of their field, lifelong specialization tends to alienate them from this broad context.

Second, many scholars publish only because they have to. Far from being a personal pleasure or an expression of professional responsibility, their work is too often a joyless mechanical exercise, emotionally weak and culturally barren.

Third, and chiefly for the reasons listed above, most academicians distinguish very sharply between publication and teaching. They ignore that at heart publication ought to be a form of teaching, continuous with, though more advanced than, the work of the classroom. The dangers inherent in the false distinction between teaching and research are clear in the style and structure of much academic publication. The average modern academician would rather convince than enlighten, rather establish a point than inspire an insight. Few scholarly journals, no matter how noble their titles, value broad and reflective approaches as much as voguish theory or data-oriented research. Such influences establish a context in which it is difficult for scholars to see their published work as coherent with their own moral concerns or ideals of teaching.

I will enlarge on these and other weaknesses of higher education in chapters to follow. For now, it should suffice to say that, at least from the perspective of true teaching set up at the start of this chapter, modern college-level instruction suffers from a disproportion between avowed purpose and effective function so broad as to inspire satire. So dramatic is this disproportion that many of the standards currently applied in questions of academic competence can be viewed, from our standard of genuine teaching, as a canon of failure.

With all this in mind, we may add one more detail to our definition of true teaching. The teacher must remain in touch, not just with one aspect of an art, but with the total art and its position in the broader context of life. By extension, the teacher must realize that, for all their apparent differences, all arts are similar in their power to evoke the desire for excellence. Only through such instruction will students understand that, rather than just a professional requisite, learning is integral to the development of their own humanity.

You might say that true teaching always results in a compound apprehension: it makes students at once conversant with a particular form of excellence and in love with excellence in general, at once excited with what they have learned and aware of an oceanic capacity to learn more. In this sense, true teaching, no matter what the subject, is a unified activity. In this latter sense, contrary to my earlier reservations, teaching *is* an art in its own right.

What sort of art? I cannot think of a better illustration than an anecdote from the life of a modern writer, Fritz Peters. As a boy, Peters was sent to a château near Paris to be educated by that famous teacher and notorious eccentric, G. I. Gurdjieff. Peters entered the master's study for the first time, expecting to learn all sorts of wonderful things. But instead of assigning books or scheduling tutorials, Gurdjieff ordered the boy to take, as his unique activity and total function, responsibility for mowing the lawns of the estate. The boy groaned but obeyed. At first the huge lawns took all his effort, but gradually he refined his technique and developed systems that would save time and improve results. He soon enjoyed his work and felt confidence in doing it well. These were feelings he had not previously had. Years later he realized that the lawn mowing had been an essential element in his education.

What sort of art — if any — did Gurdjieff practice? A possible answer may be found in the earliest extant theory of education. Plato suggested, first of all, that basic forms of understanding are inborn, and therefore that the role of the true teacher must be one of reminding as well as inculcating. Plato, moreover, saw the human frame as a microcosm that could, with proper education, reflect the beauty and order of the universe. The teacher (for example, Timaeus in Plato's dialogue of that name) acts as mediator between the order that is implicit in the cosmos and the order that is implicit in the individual.

Because of this relationship, knowledge of anything is also knowledge of oneself. If all other forms of knowledge and all arts are to have real meaning, it is only in terms of a comprehensive view that is itself predicated on a knowledge of oneself. Conversely, however, self-knowledge cannot be approached head-on but rather is available only via the channels of more specific disciplines.

With Plato in mind, we may examine the Gurdjieff episode in its proper context. While the explicit agenda of true teaching is this or that particular art, its implicit agenda is the art of self-understanding, the art of humanity. The subject of this art is the self (as defined in Chapter 11); all other arts, properly taught, point to this subject like spokes pointing to the hub of a wheel. When Gurdjieff told young Peters to mow the château lawns, he challenged the boy to discover, in a form made purer by the apparent baseness of the task, the enterprise, responsibility, drive toward order, and pure love of work that are latent in every individual. That Gurdjieff did not appeal directly to these energies, but evoked them indirectly through the mowing assignment, suggests the role of various "arts" as necessary means of appealing to the otherwise inaccessible self.

The social implications of this theory are as important as its meaning for the individual. The teaching of Socrates and Plato was two-pronged: on the one hand, they offered society the instruments of analysis that would form the basis of the scientific method; on the other, they insisted that our analytic and scientific bent be directed and qualified by self-scrutiny. The goal of such teaching was a society in which power was responsible to wisdom and what might be done was evaluated in terms of what was fit to do.

This moral fabric of knowledge was maintained by the Stoics and is also apparent in Renaissance humanism. But (with a few local exceptions) it is in disrepair today, so much so that its vestiges are generally unrecognizable. Self-knowledge has long since ceased to be a theme of philosophical inquiry, much less a topic of education. The few individuals who teach self-knowledge, or related topics, typically fall prey to accusations of narrowness and reaction from their unconsciously narrow and reactionary colleagues.

Since true teaching is not soon likely to be available on an institutional scale, we must seek it out in the writings and presence of isolated individuals. These teachers generally are not advertised as "notable" or "eminent" by their colleagues, and their published work is not often found on best-seller lists or praised in book reviews. The craft they practice is out of fashion; indeed, it has seldom been in. How will we tell them from cranks or poseurs?

In the company or with the books of true teachers, I think, we always feel a kind of shock — not the shock of a brilliant exposition but of an unsettling challenge. Whatever their subject matter or style, true teachers always convey the sense that the communication of an art demands of the student not only effort and attention but cathartic psychological change. To learn is not merely to accumulate data; it is to rebuild one's world. The autobiography of that roguish and gifted man, Benvenuto Cellini, contains the following episode:

> When I was about five years old, my father being in our small cellar ... where there was still a good fire of oak boughs ... with his viol in his hand, he played and sang to himself beside that fire. It was very cold, and as he gazed into the fire, by chance he saw in the midst of the hottest flames a little animal like a lizard, which was sporting about amidst that most scorching blaze. Having immediately perceived what it was, he caused my sister and me to be summoned, and pointing it out to us children, he gave me a violent box on the ear, at which I began to cry most excessively. Comforting me kindly, he spoke to me thus: "My dear little son, I did not give you that blow on account of anything wrong that you have done, but only that you may remember that that lizard which you saw in the fire is a salamander, a creature that has never been seen by anyone else of whom we have reliable information." So he kissed me and gave me some coppers.

This unlikely little story lends itself to an allegorical interpretation. If we take the animal in the flames to be some rare insight into nature, the father to be the conveyor of that insight, and Benvenuto the student, then the box on the ear would represent that shock which is the necessary function of true teaching. There is nothing innately shocking or awful about a real insight; rather the shock lies in the sudden juxtaposition, like a red-hot brand in water, of that insight against the way we have thought up to that moment. True teachers all seem to practice, in many ways and under many guises, this form of shock. However gentle their words or modest their demeanor, true teachers are keepers of the hot brand, masters of the beast in flames.

The shock of true teaching is evidenced by another Gurdjieff story. Traveling in Persia, the young Gurdjieff came into contact with a dervish wise man, and sat down to eat next to him. Then a student of Hatha Yoga, Gurdjieff made a practice of chewing his food as thoroughly as possible and was still carefully chewing away long after everyone else at the meal had finished. When the dervish asked him what he was up to, Gurdjieff replied confidently that he was doing it for his health. The dervish responded with a totally contrary point of view.

> "If you chew in this way as a means to health or for the sake of other attainments, then I shall have to say . . . that you have chosen the worst possible way. By chewing your food so carefully you reduce the work of your stomach. Now you are young, and everything is all right, but you are accustoming your stomach to do nothing; and when you are older, owing to the lack of normal work, your muscles will be to a certain extent atrophied. And that is bound to occur if you continue this system of chewing. . . . On the contrary, it is not at all necessary to masticate carefully. At your age it is better not to chew at all, but to swallow whole pieces, even bones if possible, to give work to your stomach."

Whether the dervish was right or wrong is not important here. Even if his opinion about eating were totally true, it would not necessarily be true teaching; as valid information, it might be communicated in a sedate book or a tedious lecture. The virtue of the wise man's response is that, whether true or false, it forced his listener to consider a viewpoint completely contrary to what he had thought before. And this new viewpoint is contrary to the old not only in its manifest conclusion (that too much chewing is unhealthy) but in its latent paradigm (how the body gains or loses health in general).

Thus the teacher forces students out of their established cognitive frames of reference, making them realize that they are able to transcend fixed perspectives, and that the process of learning demands exactly this. In this way, through shock and contradiction, the teacher may give the student practice in "mystery" and introduction to that form of discovery which is the basis of genuine achievement.

Can creativity itself be taught as an art? If we understand creative thinking as a "subject" and then compare it with other subjects like biology and mathematics, the answer would seem to be no. Creativity cannot be divided into species or expressed in axioms. Rather it is an attunement of energies and attitudes whose roots lie deep within the individual and whose principles cannot be conveyed in symbols. Yet it is possible that a good teacher, by synthesizing the shock of discovery in a student, can foster such an attunement. Good teaching develops students' creative abilities by unlocking their sense of wonder. Students learn creativity not directly from the teacher but from the cathartic self-revelation that the teacher inspires.

15 *Higher Education and Classical Wholeness*

Among the liberal arts, let us begin with the art that liberates us.

— Michel de Montaigne, *Essays*

MODERN HIGHER EDUCATION teaches millions of people to perform complex intellectual tasks, but to what extent does it teach them to think creatively? In ideology-dominated states like the USSR, higher education does not teach people (except for the scientific elite) to reason toward conclusions, but to rationalize from preestablished premises. Soviets, in other words, are first told what to think and then taught how to support and justify this dogma. Thus they are denied not only expression of free thought but access to it.

In the West we obviously fare better. But Western education, like education in the USSR, is liable to a charge of epidemic limitation and bias. In the preceding chapter I commented on a number of professional styles and practices that tend to weaken the thrust of modern teaching in the West. Now I wish to enlarge on this subject by examining the cultural attitudes that underlie these styles and practices. Paradoxically I can think of no better way to make modern issues clear than by returning to the literature of ancient Greece.

Because he is a complex figure who must orchestrate his skills to meet complex challenges, Homer's Odysseus can be regarded as the earliest example of a characteristically Western man. Unlike the other Homeric heroes, who are seldom brilliant in more than one area (Achilles, for example, is superb in the field but admits to being fuzzy in council), Odysseus is miscellaneously outstanding: prudent leader, powerful orator, eminent counselor and strategist, feared disciplinarian, major warrior, champion wrestler, runner, and hurler. He is a prince who knows the chivalry of court, the order of the town, and the regimen of the farm.

The challenges of life not only demand these skills of Odysseus but require that he mingle and temper them. In his confrontation with Circe, he functions as warrior, orator, strategist, and lover, but must repress the heroic impulse to return home and punish the suitors. When he reaches Scheria he displays athletic prowess but temporarily conceals his princely identity. Arriving at last in his native Ithaca, he conceals most of his skills and virtues under a beggar's disguise, suffering humiliation in order to test his people and surprise his enemies. By what art or skill does he make these choices? Significantly, in each case he receives instructions from the gods. But since here as elsewhere in Homer god-given virtue is viewed interchangeably with personal excellence, we may take the gods' assistance as implying a kind of higher prudence, a skill-directing skill which, indefinable in itself, defines and validates all the others. Alone in this harmonic complexity, Odysseus is the unique recipient of the curious adjective *polytropos,* "complicated," "of many turns."

The idea of a master skill, implicit in Homer, was later codified by Plato. In the *Apology* Socrates criticizes those specialists who, because they know one discipline, mistakenly believe themselves to be wise about everything. In the *Republic* and the *Symposium,* Socrates argues that a comprehensive skill is not available to us until we have mastered several disciplines. The skill that transcends all others is called dialectical and synoptic: dialectical because it depends on a universal method of analysis, synoptic because it perceives common principles at work in all the disciplines studied. Only a person both dialectical and synoptic can govern wisely. Only such a person can glimpse divine truth. The effective individual has to be a many-turned individual, not only because the arts he or she masters are mutually necessary, but also because these arts confer, as a kind of secret gift, the vision of truth and justice that is the exclusive possession of the philosophical mind.

Plato's description of the ideal curriculum leading to dialectic and synopsis (*Republic*) is the earliest surviving exposition of what we now call the liberal arts. Neither Plato nor Socrates invented this curriculum out of whole cloth; similar studies were required by their brilliant rivals, the Sophists. But while the Sophists considered the liberal curriculum to be valuable solely as preparation for a successful active life, Socrates and Plato credited it with profound political and philosophical significance. The Sophists disdained any form of learning that had no specific practical value. The Socratics, on the other hand, defended liberal disciplines as a means of transcending the specific and the practical. Only through such transcendence, they argued, could the specific and the practical be seen in their true light. Thus the Socratic idea of the *truly* "practical" is founded securely on the philosophical quest.

The position of the liberal arts in modern Western culture dramatically underlines the distinction between the Socratic and Sophistic positions. The perspective of most educators and professionals is dominated by something very like the Sophistic model. Professional education is generally aimed toward effective practice in narrowly specialized fields. Advanced graduate work and research in the humanities are intensely specialized; in the humanities, as in the natural and social sciences, only specialized expertise allows men and women to publish in most of the standard journals. The broader realm of the liberal arts is by no means despised, but is praised more or less as the Sophists praised it: we need to think analytically, to speak convincingly, to write cogently, to be well informed, because these attributes enhance our professional careers. It is pointless to seek enlightenment for itself, but highly practical to use elements of enlightenment in pursuit of success.

Far weaker in the modern mind, the Socratic educational model persists nebulously in vague and eloquent statements, usually made by college presidents and specialists emeriti, that the liberal arts establish continuity with the past, delight us, civilize us, bring us together, make us human. Such statements gladden hearts but seldom loosen purse strings. More important, they say nothing about the functioning of the human mind. Liberal education survives in most American colleges and universities as a set of generalized requirements, without an effective structure or a clear rationale. The word "dialectic" has been commandeered by Marx and his students. The word "synopsis," once designating the noblest philosophical faculty, is now applied only to summaries that shorten the labor of reading.

We might accept this state of affairs, albeit with some wistfulness, as being the way of the real world. Ironically, however, the real world does not seem to be going this way at all. Major political and personal decisions remain as interdisciplinary for us as they were for Odysseus. Indeed, the hyperspecialization of disciplines makes the necessity for interdisciplinary liaison and direction progressively more critical. No one exclusively trained in a single field can make intelligent judgments about subjects as massively interdisciplinary as abortion, energy policy, air pollution, or the insanity plea. When we compare the merits and dangers of genetic engineering, of nuclear deterrence, where is our point of reference?

It is at once galling and funny to see how, in our specialized world, such decisions are normally made. Politicians assemble in committees and call in experts to testify. Business, labor, the military, and social science contribute their insights. Natural scientists appear in force: business scientists, military scientists, government scientists, scientists from the academy. The specialists not only hold conflicting views but speak in different forms of jargon. The individual politician (if he or she has not already opted for professional success by prejudging the case along party lines) must then make a decision. The politician's staff is consulted. One staffer has been sifting the media for editorial consensus. Another has been lunching with lobbyists. A third, who has hired consultants, summarizes their report. A fourth phones in long-distance with word from the constituency. A position is hammered out in conference. A fifth staffer writes an appropriate speech, and the interdisciplinary function of politics has been fulfilled again.

Devoid of precision or creativity but nonetheless armored against catastrophe, the commonwealth lumbers on into the future. Catastrophes, however, do now and then occur, not because of a lack of assorted data but because of executive inability to evaluate the data properly. Lyndon Johnson and his staff failed conspicuously to coordinate the humanitarian, diplomatic, political, and military aspects of involvement in Vietnam. In the Watergate crisis a presidential administration disintegrated because the men at the top failed to face a question of moral responsibility. Jimmy Carter, after three years in office, declared that he was "shocked" to discover that the USSR was not single-mindedly committed to the cause of world peace. These administrations all had their staffers and consultants. What they lacked, however, was an overview or, more precisely, a sense of how various moral principles and technical disciplines are related in a comprehensive and enduring human order.

Can we connect congressional fumbling and executive blunders with inadequate grounding in the liberal arts? Such a conjecture might well cause laughter, and I, too, would join in the hilarity if we saw the liberal arts (with the Sophists) as means to specialized professional ends or (with the college presidents) as assorted links with the past that "humanize," "delight," or "bring together." Even if we accepted both these models simultaneously, with all their implications and corollaries, they would not supply an adequately dynamic connection between liberal studies and active virtue.

But the Platonic model, given the close attention it deserves, is in this regard neither weak nor laughable. Education in the *Republic* is eminently suited to active life, not only because it imparts specific skills, but for a far more compelling reason: Platonic education posits a master skill (dialectic/synopsis) as the final goal and natural product of the various specific disciplines in the liberal curriculum. This master skill can be seen not only as a kind of comprehensive prudence, tempering the application of the other skills, but also as providing a gestalt in which the other skills and the issues they address can be realistically evaluated. Beyond this, the master skill implies a philosophical dimension, a vision that addresses the bases and aims of thought and action in general.

In fullness of grasp and power of control, the educational scheme of the *Republic* is potentially more practical than the rival scheme of the Sophists, which is basically self-serving and divorced from context; moreover, the Platonic model is more detailed and effective than the good-hearted waffling of modern supporters of the humanities. Alone of all three schemes, it places liberal education within a coherent moral and political context. Alone of all three, it offers students the philosophical equivalent of Odysseus's heroic discretion.

The curriculum in the *Republic* begins with arithmetic and proceeds through plane and solid geometry to astronomy (actually, "solids in motion" or astronomy/physics). The next study, under the broad heading *mousike* (inadequately translated as "music") includes harmonics, song, dance, and literature. Dialectic comes last, bringing with it synopsis, an overview of the principles that unite all the arts. I will not concern myself here with the details, for the educational programs described in Books 3 and 7 are woven inextricably into the more complex development of the dialogue as a whole. What concerns me is the possibility that the general spirit of Platonic education can be revived in modern terms, that modern education may be reformed so as to offer, through correctly tuned interdisciplinary studies, a synoptic perspective.

Given Plato's emphasis on comprehensive education and today's educational climate, Plato might well today include chemistry and biology in his catalogue of liberal arts. Advanced study would require the mastery of foreign languages and include the social sciences and the history of ideas. Detailed versions of the curriculum might and indeed ought to vary, so long as they observe the following priorities.

A Required Core of Arts and Sciences. The variety and complexity of contemporary life, which have discouraged so many educators from requiring core curricula, ought to be seen as warning us that some common ground of discourse and inquiry must be maintained. Such a policy would ensure essential interpretive and expressive skills, continuity with the past, and cultural coherence. Equally important, it would allow for the development of individuals gifted with the ability to integrate various methods (both scientific and humanistic) in a broader perspective. Such a perspective is valuable, not only in terms of continuity but also in terms of evolution. Arguably, renewal, inspiration, even revolution, are impossible without a sense of enduring principle and historical context.

Progression from Simple to Complex. While the propensity to analyze may be inborn, the skills of analysis are not. Modern education in the humanities has too often been guilty of encouraging students to think about major philosophical and social issues before they have learned to think at all. Such methods are not only ineffective but also dangerous, especially when the subject matter is modern philosophy and literature. Much modern philosophy and literature contains sentiments that have an uncomfortable and revealing resemblance to adolescent neuroses, and that can offer a sanctimonious rationale for destructive fancies. Adolescent students would be better served by being required to take the initial steps in critical thinking than by premature contact with extreme views.

A Sense of Challenge. Influenced by the idiosyncracies of mass education, by consumer-driven models of society, by academic administrators who see higher education as "service" or "product" to be dished up to society, and by their own professional uncertainty, many professors in the liberal arts have been trying to sell their subjects to students rather than presenting them with dignity. This practice may keep bodies in the classroom, but it robs higher education of its true excitement, which lies in aspiration, toil, and self-won discovery. The professor's proper role is not that of a promoter or of anyone engaging in a transaction; it is that of one who offers a challenge. It would be better in the long run for half our university students to leave campuses and park themselves at trade schools than for teachers to persist in the commercialization of learning.

An Interdisciplinary View. Specialized courses should not be taught by "specialists" in the conventional sense of the word, but by instructors educated in principles that unite the disciplines. A professor of music history should be able to enlighten his or her students on the ties that unite music with physics (via harmonics), literature (via song and poetry), and the visual arts (via symmetry and other structural ideas). A professor of biology should give thought and time to the connections, both analogous and practical, between biology, ethics, and politics. In general, humanists should be required to achieve a fuller appreciation of the history of science and the principles of scientific inquiry, while scientists should be made much more aware of their own role within the cultural and political contexts.

Emphasis on the Quest for General Laws. All inquiry, whether scientific or humanistic, is based on the effort to resolve particular phenomena into general laws. One finds this intellectual constant even in the most heterodox social science, the wildest literary theory. Particularly in the past three decades, a number of scientists have devoted attention not only to laws that unify nature, but to principles that unify our inquiry into nature. Such investigations and initiatives (though not many scientists know it) hearken back to Plato's synoptic program and to the thought of his great antecedents, Pythagoras and Parmenides. Students should be reminded again and again of this tendency in science and of the frontiers it promises to open, especially since, with humanity facing monsters more terrible than any encountered by Odysseus, the quest for common principle and unifying goal should animate all the arts and sciences.

Education in Beauty. Scientists and humanists alike should remember to elaborate not only the truth of their discoveries but the beauty of what has been discovered. Of all the elements of learning, the perception of beauty is at once the most delightful and the most suggestive of an underlying principle that unites the disciplines. Beauty is the lingua franca of all learning and therefore must be at the core of successful pedagogy.

Preparation for Leadership. From a political perspective, one of the most conspicuous failures of modern liberal education is its almost total neglect of leadership or statesmanship as educational goals. Such famous educational programs as those of Plato and the Renaissance humanist Vittorino addressed themselves not merely to some abstract notion of enlightenment but to the fashioning of able leaders; Xenophon, Aristotle, Cicero,

Erasmus, and Castiglione all lent their efforts and eloquence to similar pedagogical ideals. That statesmanship is not an empirical "science," but an unquantifiable combination of commitment, prudence, learning, and art, did not faze these theorists in the least.

In particular, Plato and Aristotle insisted on the eclecticism of the statesman's education, with Aristotle maintaining that leaders had to be interdisciplinary because they would ultimately administer all arts and sciences. Though the lack of such theory and such programs today may be explained by political and historical factors, it is nonetheless inexcusable. There is no more obvious sign that our modern age, so liberal, enlightened, and self-conscious, is in fact moving into the future blindfold.

An Implicit Program of Self-understanding. I have spoken of the unique importance of self-knowledge both as an index of our human reality and as the inevitable by-product of all great teaching. Professors should be reminded, intellectually and materially, that the quest for self-knowledge is an elemental principle of liberal studies, that self-knowledge is a goal upon which liberal studies rightly converge. To lose sight of this goal in a thicket of exigeses, case studies, and theoretical manifestos is to fail at one of the primary functions of teaching.

Our original question, then, has a twofold answer. Conceived in terms of the scholarly and pedagogical programs in place, the liberal arts are sharply limited as means of promoting creative and independent thought. Recast, on the other hand, in terms of a synoptic theory of inquiry, the liberal arts might be not only useful but transfiguring as vehicles of enlightenment and social evolution. The implementation of such a theory would require a comprehensive reorganization of curricula, both on the undergraduate level and in the more advanced education of future professors. It would suggest, in addition, a radical reevaluation of the nature and purpose of academic research.

16 Vision, Learning, and Power

> But if the specialist is ignorant of the inner philosophy of the science he cultivates, he is much more radically ignorant of the historical conditions requisite for its continuation; that is to say: how society and the heart of man are to be organized in order that there may continue to be investigators.
>
> — José Ortega y Gasset, *The Revolt of the Masses*

THE WAYS of creativity are infinite; the ways of formal learning are numbered. Restless, curious, playful, contriving, the innovative mind feeds on challenge and makes its home in the province of mystery. It ensnares the force of nature in an airy net of words and signs, and when caught in the toils itself, it designs new language to regain its freedom. One can no more set limits for mind than one can trap starlight in a bag or convince a yearling not to run. Formal learning, on the other hand, covers but small bands of this colossal spectrum. Rather than being free, scholarship is governed by social necessity and professional tradition; stylized and departmentalized, it proliferates in coteries. Its byword is not challenge but commodity.

This contradiction stems from the political-economic priorities of the West. Look at the two major dimensions of academic activity, teaching and research. As we have seen, the primary function of Western undergraduate teaching is to fashion individuals who are economically viable. The "professional" majors — pre-med, psychology, economy, computer science, and so forth — are funnels through which the academy supplies the practical needs of culture; the apparently less goal-driven majors — English, history, philosophy, foreign languages — are valued as gateways, variously, to law, publishing, communications, primary or secondary education, and careers in the university itself.

Such professions make up a departmentalized society that is the archetype of the departmentalized university, to which the university is precisely suited. The "liberal" undergraduate degree requirements are supposed to supply an intellectual breadth that transcends professional interests. But in general these requirements are relatively weak and incoherent. Rather than a blueprint for intellectual freedom, they are usually little more than a garnish to specialization.

The political-economic foundations of research, though less obvious, are equally secure. By far the most impressive research enterprise in history — the enterprise that serves as a model for all others — is modern natural science. Natural science is often referred to as being "disinterested" or "pure"; but these congratulatory terms are inaccurate for two important reasons.

First, as I have tried to show in Parts 1 and 2, science is influenced by the same psychological and ethical forces that apply to creativity of other kinds, hence it has no greater claim to "purity" than they.

Second, society does not support science out of mere curiosity. Science, instead, is the spearhead of an ongoing and comprehensive effort to enlarge human power and safeguard human welfare in a challenging physical environment and a competitive arena of species. In order to appreciate the power orientation of natural science, one need only compare the amount of money supplied in grants to projects with medical, military, or other technological implications with the amount supplied for environmental or philosophical scientific research. We hear many critics, including scientists, inveighing against the use of science by the military to create more weapons and more powerful weapons. In a larger sense, however, all scientists are soldiers, enlarging human dominions with that most powerful of known weapons, the mind.

This sense of conquest and elemental power gives certain fields in natural science a dynamic and even heroic quality. At present, few would dispute the claim that scientific research offers opportunities for true innovation matched in few other professions. But this intensity is offset by an equally dramatic narrowing of perspective. In the context of natural science itself, the ascendancy of science as power has occurred at the expense of such less "profitable" aspects of science as environmentalism, professional self-scrutiny, and pure contemplation. The vision of science is focused far more on the advancement of human material interests than on the global balance of nature or on the delight of understanding. Science has taken on the power of the gods, with little effort to acquire their wisdom.

Concentration of support for cost-effective scientific projects not only constricts (and to my mind, demeans) the character of scientific research. In addition, it depletes the blood supply of nonscientific disciplines — history, art, the humanities. These non-power-related branches of inquiry have not been totally abandoned. Instead they have been informed, in the eloquent language of the dollar sign, that they have little cultural priority.

What is the state of research in the nonscientific fields? Consider the humanities. Because these fields of inquiry lie outside the natural food chain of the economy, they must be funded artificially, through state allocations and grants from public and private agencies. Such aid is given because expert teachers in large number are needed to maintain the Western commitment to "liberal" undergraduate education. Since liberal education is a prerequisite for professional viability, and since it conforms to various shared ideals concerning enlightenment and excellence, it is "carried" by the Western economy. And by virtue of these ideals, humanistic educators are expected, as a sign of their own excellence and enlightenment, to pursue and publish their own research.

For these reasons the humanities, though lacking the wealth and dynamism of the natural sciences, are still alive and kicking. Many contemporary scholars in the humanities are as productive, in terms of quantity, as their scientific counterparts; their research is published by dozens of university presses and hundreds of academic journals. Like scientists, humanists log millions of miles per year en route to and from meetings of learned societies; like scientists, they are accorded honor and promotion proportionally to the volume and the perceived quality of their publications.

Given such security and freedom from market pressures, it would seem that scholars in the humanities would range freely among ideas, exploring innovative opportunities, meditating on the human condition, reviewing academic priorities, chiding society for its foibles and reminding it of its responsibilities. But while a few outstanding scholars do indeed engage in such activities, the majority do not.

The reasons for this failure stem, I think, from the traditions and priorities of the modern academy. Most humanists are constitutionally wary of undertaking social criticism or making value judgments in general. They have been nursed on an academic tradition that prizes technique and distrusts values. Trained as specialists, they are insensitive to interdisciplinary connections and leery of broad issues. They have been taught by modern culture, especially by empirical science, that because questions of value are unquantifiable, they are irrelevant to research. They have exchanged the opportunity for moral inquiry and commitment for an illusion of objectivity, a frozen equipoise.

The dynamics of humanistic publication militate against spirited and creative enterprise. In the natural sciences, the reproducibility of results and the precision of communication make judgments regarding excellence a relatively easy task. In humanistic discourse, there is no such thing as certainty or reproducibility or precise communication. The question of whether a given humanist's work is excellent or adequate or flawed must therefore be decided in terms of the number and rank of other humanistic scholars he or she is able to impress. This state of affairs discourages bold advances and disciplinary self-questioning (especially in younger scholars), instead encouraging conservative projects, patriarchism, faddism, and groupiness. It paves the way for a politicization of scholarship, a damper on free inquiry.

Instead of developing an open forum, these factors have nurtured a bureaucracy of letters, a vast system of categories, departments, and subspecialties devoted to narrow and formalized discourse, inimical to questions of wholeness, and resistant to any evolution except the incremental proliferation of its own complexity.

These conditions condemn the humanistic academy, not only to uncertainty as to its own direction, but also to a debilitating loss of scope. In terms of the human topics with which intelligent people might expectably be concerned, humanistic research is more exclusive than inclusive. Philosophy has all but abdicated (in favor of the social sciences) its old realms of psychology and politics; it has silently and totally withdrawn its old claim to be sovereign interpreter of all the other arts and sciences. Literary research, in the main, involves itself with stylistic, theoretical, and historical niceties; it routinely evades the great questions that literature treats. History breeds on change and generally ignores the question of what is permanent. Holistic, philosophical perspectives get lip service in all these fields, but they cut no mustard with the university presses and journals whose editorial boards determine professional success or failure.

Forgotten by the humanities, or lost in the interstices between their specialties, are the classic issues of civilized life. How may we best plan, or renew, a city? How may we educate a leader? How ought we to treat our natural environment? Is there a morality of science? What is the nature of the family? What is the meaning of terms like "freedom," "responsibility," "courage"? Are the learned disciplines unified or disparate? Disregarded by the humanistic disciplines is the initiative that would uniquely validate them: the attempt to write and to teach about the major questions of human experience.

Disregard for truly substantive questions translates into disdain for the uniquely philosophical minds that are drawn to them. Just as the modern university has no time for the most important human subjects, it has, ironically, no place on its faculty for the brightest people.

For these reasons, the humanities find themselves between two stools. On the one hand, they lack the economic viability and frontier heroics of the natural sciences; on the other, they lack the integrity of a discipline committed to moral enlightenment and reform. Neither fish nor fowl, neither the hand that strikes nor the conscience that restrains, they convey no social urgency and must therefore depend on the modest charities of an otherwise occupied state.

AN INNOVATIVE ACADEMY

Can we expect some improvement? Present trends are not strong enough to allow for anything more than fanciful speculation. Instead let me describe some of the conditions that might operate in a research institution whose goal was real discovery rather than market viability. Such an institution would have as its basis neither a responsibility to students nor a debt to progress, but a community of excellent minds. Its goal would be neither the mere advancement of human power nor the undifferentiated acquisition of learning, but self-knowledge in the broadest sense of the word.

Research time and teaching time would be shared equally by all faculty, regardless of their specialties. There would be no "departments," but a much more informal and flexible assortment of substructures, including colleges, "centers," and discussion groups. Such groups would welcome participants from other specialties, not out of hospitality, but in an effort to freshen and enrich their own fields.

Aspiring humanists would be (as natural scientists are) severely tested in terms of technical and conceptual expertise. Required of all humanists, regardless of their period, would be reading mastery of at least one ancient and one modern language, conversance with philosophical methodology, classical philology, and the history of ideas (including natural science). Required of all humanists would be the cultivation of "creative" expertise (poetry, fiction, informal essay).

At such a university, no subject of real interest to humanity or relevance to the natural environment would be considered unsuitable for study, but narrow and oversophisticated researches would be dismissed as trivial. Among professors, positions of highest respect and authority would be accorded to philosophers whose specialty was inquiry into the shape of knowledge as a whole; these "specialists" would not only pursue their own research but conduct colloquia for their colleagues. Next in order of precedence would be the philosophy of government (conceived not only in terms of traditional politics but as a necessary human skill in the preservation of environmental balance) and the philosophy of art, including literature, the visual and performing arts, aesthetics.

For these utopian humanists, publication (as it is for scientists) would be virtually automatic. The readership at large, not some editorial board, would decide which publications were worthy of widespread dissemination and which were not. Electronic methods of publication, transmission, and indexing would reduce the paper glut and make relevant materials easier to acquire. All major publications in any field would be accompanied by essays, written by the professors themselves, explaining the material in nontechnical language and outlining its significance to inquiry at large.

Education at this academy would be based on a bibliography/exam model rather than a course-work model, freeing faculty to lecture on subjects of their own choice. Faculty, however, would regularly give introductory lectures dealing with the basic principles of their fields. These lectures, as well as the bibliographies and examinations, would conform with the pedagogical principles outlined in Chapter 15. When feasible, students would assist faculty in their research, thus getting to know their professors as models of inquiry rather than just sources of information.

I mention such a university in passing not as a manifesto for radical reform, but in order to demonstrate the extent to which the university as traditionally instituted is removed from the phenomenon of personal discovery and the forces of cultural renewal. It seems improbable that modern higher education could reform itself along the lines I recommend. But it can improve its active influence by recognizing more fully its own equivocal position in society, by reworking its infrastructures to allow for increased flexibility, and by reevaluating its principles and goals of research.

EVOLUTION AND INTEREST

Let us look at an argument that is the reverse of much that has been said in this and the two preceding chapters.

True, modern higher learning is more innovative in some fields than in others. True, this disproportion at root is caused by historical cultural priorities. But how can it be otherwise? The uniting goals of individual and group, of the whole human project, are power and security. Every conscious step in progress is conceived as being toward these goals. To seek to control or reform or purify this process artificially would be in effect to put a lid on the economy; it would at once hamper the development of material power and decrease the largess that material power freely contributes to the arts and the humanities. Look at ancient Athens, Renaissance Italy, Tudor England, and you will see the arts and humanities deriving extraordinary benefits from the flow of free markets. Even the Sophistic education, which you decry as being shortsighted, is a powerful channel of economic development and deserves its central position in higher learning.

This materialist counterargument must be considered seriously because the views it puts forth, no matter what we think or say, are overwhelmingly likely to prevail. Ideas that offer power will be favored in the future as they have been in the past; thinkers will be, as they have been and are, paid to think about subjects that are dear to the payers' hearts. But the very historical periods cited — ancient Greece, Renaissance Italy, and sixteenth-century England — suggest that this materialist interpretation cannot fully explain the process of innovation. Even though great intellectual innovations do spring from power, they spring *away* from power, exploiting substance for idea, transmuting their own material bases into a thousand inspired and fantastic shapes. Thus, while the work of Plato, da Vinci, or Shakespeare can be causally explained in terms of economic factors, such an explanation falls short of appreciating the new freedoms that these innovative minds uncovered.

It is equally important to note that a major feature of each of these great historical periods was methodological and educational reform, implemented respectively by figures like Socrates and Plato, Vittorino da Feltre and Guarino Veronese, and Sir John Cheke and Roger Ascham; and that these reforms, in each case, moved strongly toward integrated interdisciplinary knowledge and highlighted the study of government. In these areas we find not only positive endorsements of material power (for example, the Sophists, Machiavelli, Bacon) but critical reassessments of it (Socrates, Castiglione, Thomas More). Historically, then, the argument of power may work, but rightly understood, it suggests that power naturally fulfills itself, not in undifferentiated expansion, but in intellectual revolution and the freedom of thought. If creativity indeed rises in apprenticeship to material power, its goals, nonetheless, are not determined by its origin.

17 *Philosophy and the Equation of Being*

But a woman in threadless gold
Burns us with the brushings of her dress
And a dissociated abundance of being.

— Wallace Stevens,
"The Woman in Sunshine"

The mind, that ocean where each kind
Does straight its own resemblance find.

— Andrew Marvell,
"The Garden"

IT MAY BE SAID that every creative achievement or innovative insight is a philosophical act, and that the pursuit of such achievements and insights, practiced continuously and single-heartedly, turns the pursuer into a kind of philosopher. I wish to examine this statement with special reference to the following questions: In what sense is creativity "philosophical," and what can the study of creativity tell us about philosophy?

Suppose that the natural subject of creative thinking is form. Other sorts of thought may list details, dream, memorize, opine, harangue, rationalize, and so forth, but the special province of creative thought is to perceive and communicate form. Suppose that by "form" we mean the operative principle of a given phenomenon, not only in terms of internal structure but also in terms of the relation of that phenomenon to an inclusive context. Creative thinking cleaves to this principle and regards all else as ancillary to it. Creative thinking is philomorphic (form-loving).

Suppose, too, that the natural subject of philosophy is truth. Other professions may be happy with appearances; they may seek power, money, pleasure, or benefit to society. But the sovereign motive of philosophy is to discover as much as possible about what *is* and in so doing to distinguish elemental being from illusions, lies, and mere details. In the process of discovery, philosophy, more than any other profession, relies on the procedure known as abstraction — the refinement of raw data into coherent ideas and the organization of individual ideas into more inclusive categories. Because successive levels of abstraction lead to more and more general and dominant ideas, and because in all philosophical fields what is true is identified with what holds generally, the process of abstraction, properly developed, is also the discovery of truth.

It follows that the relation of philosophy to creativity stands or falls on the relation of form to truth, as both words have been specially defined above. This relation lies in the fact that form as "operative principle" belongs as a subset to the category of abstractions that philosophy addresses. Form as defined here is what Aristotle termed "formal cause" or shaping principle. It is what gives identity — independent being — to an object, event, or idea. As such, form is an inevitable goal in the philosophical search for truth.

This explains why it is possible to say that innovative vision, no matter what its subject matter, is a philosophical act. We might say that the act of vision is a single step in what a philosopher would imagine to be a process of many steps, or that philosophy as rightly practiced is a sequence of acts of vision. The individual whose vision is subordinated to a nonphilosophical goal — the cure of a disease, the composition of a poem, the foundation of a state — practices truncated philosophy. The individual who seeks vision for itself and is inspired by each successful step to search for the next is a philosopher.

These relations, between the words "form" and "truth" and between creativity and philosophy, suggest a question whose ramifications occupy the rest of this chapter: Does form or shaping principle have a "shape" of its own? In other words, are the operative principles of all being endlessly different or basically unified?

To this big question I would like to propose the following answer: that forms are similar because our concept of "being" (and hence of "truth") has itself implicit form.

What sort of form? In science, as in interpretation of all sorts, the major role of the verb *to be* is the expression of equivalency. This role is implicit in what is perhaps the most powerful single symbol yet produced by humanity, the equal sign — "=." The "=" has form because it unequivocally conveys a symmetry between the expressions on either side of it. This symmetry cannot help but be profoundly symbolic. It suggests the translatability of experience from one type of signification to another and, by extension, the translating power of mind. It suggests that mind itself, both consciously and unconsciously, is equivalent to and symmetrical with outside experience. Hence the "=" is symbolic of Mind itself, while the innumerable symmetries it controls, from mathematics and physics to music and dream, correlate deeply and beautifully with the symmetries of nature.

Of course, equivalency is not the only type of being. The verb *to be* is essential in designating attributes (hot, white), in making comparisons, in determining space/time locality, in establishing category and limit, and so on. But only being-as-equivalency suggests total definition and therefore complete existence. The symmetrical concept of being is at the heart of all interpretation, so to this extent the intelligible dimension of being, which we call truth, can be said to have form.

If we accept as our hypothesis that truth is symmetrical and thus has form, then a number of interesting corollaries follow. We may propose, first of all, that the model of truth as equivalency/symmetry, possibly inborn but at least learned with language, serves as a permanent psychological matrix, which is not only receptive and appreciative, but sculptural and creative. As *receiver*, the matrix evaluates all experience, sorting through miscellaneous phenomena in search of its own symmetry. Phenomena that lack or seem to lack symmetry are rejected as incoherent; phenomena that seem to possess it are apprehended, discovered as discrete entities. As *creator*, the matrix supplies, as it were, the idea of an idea, serving variously as the inspiring impulse and shaping principle of ideas, and as the pattern against which they may be tested.

In Part I I described, and loosely interconnected, five processes that involved the perception of form: inspiration, discovery, analysis, imagination, and the appreciation of beauty. It is conceivable that these processes have, as root principle and common denominator, a matrix of symmetry like that here described. We see scientists expressing symmetry in equations, poets in metaphor, composers and artists in evocatively balanced structures; but beneath all this we see the philomorphic mind seeking its own symmetries in ways that cannot fairly be distinguished in terms of dichotomies like rational/irrational or empirical/intuitive.

Such a theory would account for the otherwise uncanny similarities between insights of all sorts — personal, scientific, humanistic, and artistic — in terms of their psychological effect on the perceiver. It would account for the opinion, put forth logically by philosophers like Plato and Leibniz and expressed more sentimentally by countless others, that all knowledge is unified.

The close association of form with truth and being also suggests that phenomena that convey strong and coherent formal principles may in so doing produce a more dynamic impression of pure being than phenomena in which form is partial or obscure. Viewed in these terms, intense intellectual, aesthetic, or even emotional delight — our wonderment at an idea or work of art or example of human beauty — is also existential delight: the thrill of closer-than-normal contact with pure being. At the head of this chapter I quoted lines from a Wallace Stevens poem about such an experience. It is worth looking at this poem in full.

The Woman in Sunshine

It is only that this warmth and movement are like
The warmth and movement of a woman.
It is not that there is any image in the air
Nor the beginning nor end of a form:
It is empty. But a woman in threadless gold
Burns us with the brushings of her dress
And a dissociated abundance of being,
More definite for what she is —
Because she is disembodied,
Bearing the odors of summer fields,
Confessing the taciturn and yet indifferent,
Invisibly clear, the only love.

The poem does not describe a "physical" woman in sunshine. Instead it suggests that "something" about the sunshine elicits the erotic, "burning" presence of a woman, and that simultaneously evoked, as a kind of abstract "abundance," is a philosophical insight into "being." The triple metaphorical equation, the identification of atmospheric "warmth and movement" (here a summer breeze) with "a woman in threadless gold" and "a dissociated abundance of being" implies a scheme in which perceived nature, personal sexuality, and metaphysical truth partake of common principle and hence can be translated into each other. It implies a kind of passionate heuristic in which the love of beauty is also the love of truth ("the only love"). It asserts the same unity of emotion with idea that I described in the chapter Integrity. Stevens, who speaks of the sunlit phenomenon as lacking physical "form," is nonetheless presenting (through an elegant poetic structure of his own), the formal principles that shape and motivate poetic creativity.

"The Woman in Sunshine" suggests the ancient teaching that artists' efforts to communicate to others the world that they see should be characterized by a formal integrity that mimics the integrity of the things they describe. Such reasoning, perhaps, explains what is for many the uniquely satisfying effect of classical sculpture and architecture. In its balance and symmetry, in its sense of just proportion and untroubled simplicity, classical art may be seen as teaching us, or reminding us of, the formal principles that underlie all cognition.

For many ancient artists, moreover, the aesthetic concern for pure form was synonymous with a concern for nature. Plato supplied a theoretical basis for this equation when he wrote in the *Timaeus* that nature itself was a visible model of divine being. He took a similar line in the *Phaedrus,* maintaining that verbal art should imitate the structure of a living thing. Such concern for formal integrity in interpretation is not limited to ancient times, or to the arts alone. In mathematics, in which a single proposition can often be proved or disproved in a variety of ways, the palm for elegance is always awarded to the simplest demonstration, and in physics, whose experts base their judgments on the same standards, simplicity is seen as suggesting not only human ingenuity but the surpassing elegance of nature itself.

The symmetrical model of being and truth, on the other

hand, suggests major problems inherent in some types of inquiry and basic distinctions between modes of understanding. In the natural sciences, equivalency (=) can often be rendered with such precision that the process of scientific description is little short of the reconstruction of nature. Through such a process, for example, we may send space probes in and out of the orbits of distant planets, alter genetic inheritances, and invoke the power of solar fusion. For science, in other words, precise epistemological symmetry is so common that its almost magical power is all but taken for granted.

Description in the arts and the humanities may be said to have much the same aim as description in the sciences: accuracy. But in these fields another condition obtains. The arts and humanities describe reality by means of necessarily ambiguous words, images, and symbols. Rich and evocative as the process may be, it allows for no precise equivalency, and hence no foolproof measure. To describe a phenomenon — a tree, a kiss — in language or clay or brush strokes is not to reconstruct it in reality but rather to convey an approximation of perception or intent. Linguistic approximations on simple levels (STOP signs, for example), may be relatively accurate communicators, but the gap between subject and description widens as the subjects described become more complex. The verb *to be* cannot command the power of "=," try as it may for such dominion. The drama of philosophy resides specifically in the frustrated straining of language to reconstruct the world, and the farce of ideology springs from the illusion that language has succeeded.

The gap between scientific and nonscientific experience widens as we move from the realm of pure inquiry to the realm of practice. The precision of scientific description ensures in many operations that the gap between theory and practice is virtually nonexistent. In other words, the description of an event can, in these cases, be used to produce an identical event. In nonscientific experience, with its inevitable disjunction between description and event, no such reproducibility exists. A moralist can spend a whole career breathing vigor into the Golden Rule without the certainty that the effort has improved a single life. A single tenet of the Bill of Rights, phrased in what seems a triumph of clarity and accuracy, can spawn generations of interpretive conflict.

Hence there arise two basic distinctions between scientific and nonscientific inquiry: First, nonscientific inquiry, whether addressed to the interpretation of a poem or the preservation of a city, is through the theory/practice dichotomy forever at one remove from the human reality it wishes to shape. While scientists can touch their own reality with bare hands, poets and philosophers must stand some distance away from theirs, like boardwalk gamesters who use levers to pick up the ring with the steel hook.

Second, the precise description and communication of modern science have made possible a form of progress denied to nonscientific fields. Natural scientists sit on the shoulders of their predecessors and can claim to be participants in a continual advance. Poets and philosophers, on the other hand, are condemned by the nature of their calling to face, century after century, the same basic issues. In this sense, poets and philosophers are frozen in history, and it is in immobility, rather than in any illusion of progress, that they must see their unique challenge.

From these rooted distinctions have arisen, in modern times, the widely recognized separation between scientific and humanistic pursuits and even between the psychologies of those who follow them. In the minds of many, their separation has become as generic as that between birds and fish. The strict division of disciplines from secondary school on, and the radical specialization of modern professions, ensure that the sense of distinctness will be inherited and maintained in some form or other by the young.

Yet there are reasons for asking whether such a separation is fully justifiable and indeed whether it is healthy. These reasons derive, first of all, from the fact that, while precision in achieving mental symmetries varies widely among the disciplines, the passion for symmetry dominates all thought. Poet and scientist, lawmaker and engineer, to the extent that they work honestly, seek similar symmetries in their attempts to do mental justice to the world around them. Differences in language, variations in results, should not obscure the unity of the quest.

Second, as I sought to show in Part 1, the operation of creative thought in the arts and sciences has too many common principles to allow for categorical distinctions between one field and another. These links are both methodological and psychological.

Methodological. Contemporary science, along its cutting edge if not among its rank and file, is in the process of questioning its own uniqueness. In the late work of Gregory Bateson and the writings of Edward Wilson, Ilya Prigogine, Lewis Thomas, and Stephen Jay Gould, among others, can be found a variety of efforts to redefine science as a process involving poetic insight and aiming at philosophical vision. Implicit in much of their work (as it was in the earlier writings of Alfred North Whitehead and Michael Polanyi) is the argument that precise measurement and description are of little avail except in the company of creative energy, personal commitment, and (as Gould puts it) "global intuition." This line of thinking would give some support to my own claim that strong cognitive bonds link the experience of all individuals — scientists, humanists, or poets — who love form and seek to distinguish truth from falsehood.

Psychological. It is a modern belief, epidemic in the lay public and seldom discouraged by scientists themselves, that modern science "does" special things in special ways, and that scientists are special people. Such a statement might be true of master scientists, in whom a combination of talent, energy, and experience produces uncanny insights. But from this criterion, one might say with equal justice that great violinists and novelists and architects do special things in special ways. Achievement in any profession requires a combination of logical understanding, technical skill, intuition, and pure love. Achievement in any field requires a balance of head and heart too subtle to be quantified. Showing that a type of thinking is exclusively scientific or exclusively nonscientific is as impossible as cutting a magnet into a positive half and a negative half. "Educating" young people to be exclusively scientific or exclusively artistic is a tyranny which, insofar as it is effective, produces deadheaded scientists and impotent artists.

If similarities and distinctions of so complex a nature obtain among the disciplines, and if understanding these similarities and distinctions is of such importance to our own renewal, it follows that we might benefit from trying to develop a "bracketing" discipline that seeks systematically to address exactly these subjects. This putative discipline would do more than compare methodologies. It would endeavor to build a comprehensive model of inquiry; it would point out areas of redundancy, weakness, or neglect; it would set and preserve standards. "Philosophical" in the strongest sense of the word, this discipline would seek "form" in the communal and historical structure of mind. And here, as in every other discipline, the examination of existing forms will reveal the possibility of new ones. If it accepts the challenge and broadens its exploration to this formidable scope, philosophy can be a force of innovation.

18 Art

And art itself may be defined as a single-minded attempt to render the highest kind of justice to the visible universe, by bringing to light the truth, manifold and one, underlying its every aspect.

— Joseph Conrad, Preface to *The Nigger of the "Narcissus"*

PROFESSIONAL CIRCUMSTANCE recently threw me into contact with the work of about fifty of America's most active young poets. Over a period of about two months, some book of poetry was almost always open on my desk, and sometimes stacks of those books stood so high that they threatened to engulf me.

During this time I was also snatching a morning here and there to work on this book. It did not occur to me for weeks that my two jobs were intimately connected with each other. Here I am, writing about creativity, and what's more creative than a poet? Even the name poet comes from the Greek "to create." Can I learn nothing about creativity from this abundance of artistic creation?

With this question in mind, I thoroughly reconsidered what I had been reading. The very abundance was dizzying. Three decades ago, poets were few and far between, and the idea of actually making a living as a poet was considered almost insane. Writing poetry was held to be an act of love, a bold initiative of spirit taken with little hope of material gain. Today, however, there are thousands of professional poets active in America. Their presence owes itself to the sudden rise of creative writing programs at American colleges and universities. They teach poetic composition to the young and are expected to display their talents in print.

This development has obvious advantages. Creative writing is a welcome and most appropriate new subject in liberal education. Tenured, fully salaried positions on American campuses give poets new security. But, ironically, these benefits carry serious drawbacks. Poetry, which used to be a delightfully amateur thing to do, has become professionalized and is taking on, to some extent, the homogeneity and dreary respectability of the other professions. The risk of writing poetry is gone, and with it the passion that dares risks. Poets no longer write out of the urgent necessities of spirit; they write to maintain professional output. And totally lacking in this output is a quality available only in the gifted amateur: an eclecticism that focuses in poetry the many aspects, some harmonious, some contradictory, of a varied and active life.

The professionalization of poetry may also account for striking similarities among all the poems I read. Though there was much variety in terms of subject matter, the poets were nearly unanimous in avoiding many of the stylistic and psychological elements typical of more traditional verse. Few poems reminded me of normal human speech or were understandable without major effort. Few poems told a story or vividly described nature. Few poems had a formal structure of any sort. Few poems were based on folk themes or classical myth or legend, and few poems reminded me of song or ritual or any of the acknowledged ancient sources of poetry. Few poems openly expressed anger or veneration or moral judgment. Few poems directly conveyed joy.

Granted, there were exceptions. Two poets in particular developed strong and enriching ties with the ethnic past and did so in language that carried the power of honest speech. But even these poets, I felt, were impeded rather than empowered by the puritanical prohibitions of modern free-verse style. Though not all American poets write this way (Richard Wilbur and the late Robert Penn Warren, for example, have worked successfully with traditional forms), the exclusions listed above suggest the general character of contemporary poetry. Instead of being recognizable poetic art, it is reconstituted prose, resembling normal prose in everything except its uneven shape and its mannered mystifications. It has generally renounced its ancient sources of strength, and the results, generally, are anxious, timid, and frail.

The exposition that follows is an effort to explain what brought us to this pass, not only in poetry but in other arts as well. It is an effort to convey the urgent and dynamic character of creativity in ancient art, and to measure the enormous distance between the ancient character and "art" as currently practiced.

What is the nature of creativity in art? To answer this question fairly, we must look beyond current views of art and artists, back to primitive art and its influence on the classics. We must appreciate anew the universal necessity for art: why generically similar art forms have arisen in every culture, and why patterns of artistic development in cultures isolated from one another have followed similar courses. Only in terms of historical perspective, I believe, can we rightly understand the present position of art and the challenges facing artists.

What, then, was the historical necessity, the evolutionary purpose, of art? Although art performs many functions and springs from many impulses, I submit that its original role was to make the process of communal living important to its audience. To be sure, this flies in the face of the normal assumption that art is an expression of things already accepted as important — gods, coronations, the hunt, war, planting and harvest, the seasons, love, childbirth, death; but the mere expression of things already recognized as important is not an urgent enough motivation to justify the universal cultural eminence of art. Like all other human activities, ancient art is expressive, but more important, it is ethical and hortatory. It reminds societies of the needs that bind them together and of the special institutions that meet their needs. It is an effective and relatively painless way of making individuals remember their communal origins, the environmental threats that face them, the drama of the great passages in their lives, and the richness of their shared values.

Even in primitive societies, such typical subjects of art are more easily underestimated or forgotten than we might think. The truly important events in life are generally specialized to social subgroups (childbirth, hunting, healing, priesthood, leadership) or so broadly cyclical as to be easily put out of mind (the seasons, floods, planting and harvest, death). When these events occur, they are accorded close attention, but as they do not often occur, and do not always occur to all, they are soon forgotten and, of greater significance, never integrated in a coherent image of communal life. It is exactly by turning occasional events into permanent presences, by unequivocally establishing their importance, that art makes communal life important to its audience.

What is the process by which art renders life important, communal, and coherent? The best word for this process is celebration. "Celebration" comprehends both the primitive religious function of art as ritual and the secular role of art as a medium of delight. In ancient art these two functions apparently were fused and did not admit of discrete definitions, hence the appropriateness of the single word, the old word, "celebration."

Yet not all definitions of the word will do. Art is not celebration in the sense that celebration implies giddiness or victory.

The sense of the word meant here is one of a ritual whose pleasure is derived from the idea of doing justice to an otherwise elusive or oppressive reality. The experience of doing justice is conversely the experience of being relieved of a burden, and, as Aristotle taught, the sense of unburdenment is pleasurable whether it is achieved through laughter or through tears.

How does art achieve the act of justice? Plato and Aristotle characterized this process as mimesis, imitation. Like the magic that calls forth a genie, imitation evokes and makes immediate the classic events of life and the primary factors of the human condition. Both Plato and Aristotle were aware that art ought not to imitate individual things and actions so much as to imitate their underlying ideas. One might say, for example, that a camera "imitates" the light and darkness it confronts. A good artist, on the other hand, imitates the very idea of light and darkness and the internal idea of the forms whose external shape the light reveals. An imitation of an idea may also be called a translation of an idea or a metaphor for it. Thus creative art establishes a symmetry between idea and form and holds true to the beauty/justice model and the "equation of being" matrix.

Because such imitation is necessarily sophisticated, requiring symbolic understanding and technical excellence, we may fairly define artistic imitation as "interpretive" rather than "graphic." Truly celebratory art maintains, as part of its emotive power, an analytic and inquiring faculty that opens the artist to inspiration and discovery. Art does not dignify the routine so much as reveal the remarkable: the hidden wonder that persists in all great human events and in the rituals that surround them. It is through such a revelation, when the technical details of art unite to communicate some pure idea of things, that we experience in art the transforming presence of beauty.

Here then is a tentative answer to the question, What is the nature of creativity in art? Artistic creativity is vision of the ideas that brood behind the surface of human experience. This vision is necessary for the process of interpretive imitation (that is, artistic creation), which is itself necessitated by society's elemental desire to celebrate life. Society must celebrate life in order to accept life and succeed at life. Society cannot celebrate life effectively unless its means of celebration conveys knowledge of the ideas behind life and provokes the passionate experience of beauty.

Is art supposed to teach us something? If art is anything like what I describe, the question becomes absurd. Art is nothing if not teaching, for it teaches us, in various ways and on various levels, about nature, about ideas, about ourselves, and about itself. The artist who rejects teaching rejects art.

One final question: How does classic art differ from primitive art? Classic art, the art of a Sophocles or a Michelangelo, occurs in advanced cultures that recognize religious and political functions as distinct from each other, and recognize distinctions (as Plato and Aristotle did) between physical reality and the province of ideas. In other words, classic art occupies a world that admits of philosophy both as a pursuit distinct from religious experience and as a method of refining particulars into universals.

Classic art is itself philosophical. Freed from religious constraint and occurring only in cultures in which systematic analysis is prized, classic art can examine as well as celebrate culture, focusing on the intricately connected framework that supports advanced society, and on the subtle dangers that threaten it. Thus the creation of classic art necessitates a kind of distancing between artists and their social context: a separation allowing perspective. Typical of critical separation is the form of negative justice-doing that expresses itself in satiric art. But even here the distancing stops short of total divorce. If simple celebratory art reiterates the importance of shared values, satiric art admonishes us that these values are in danger. For all its acumen and self-consciousness, classic art retains an element of the ancient spirit: the urge to celebrate, rather than ignore or reject, the essential phenomena of shared humanity.

To accept these premises is to arrive at some surprising conclusions about art. To begin with, what can we make of the common-sense distinctions between art, on the one hand, and reality or life or nature on the other? Viewing art, as we just have viewed it, as a basic evolutionary force means understanding that these customary distinctions do not necessarily hold. Art is a primal strength, a communal impulse. It is a language holding society together by stronger cords than the mere language of words. It lives in harmony not with the alien surfaces of things but with their inner spirit, their intimately familiar ideas. It bears these ideas into our awareness and makes us participate in them. It knows us not as individuals with names but as a single awareness, receptive and unified. And as the language of interior humanity, it is one of the very few available means to self-knowledge.

Admittedly, all this sounds like lots of books about how to appreciate art or those television documentaries on art whose purpose is to make Rodin yet more profound or Leonardo yet more enigmatic. Admittedly, our day-to-day experience of art, through movies, books, domestic decorations, refresher courses, is somewhat less dynamic. Moreover, "modern" art, with its irresolvable abstractions, its asymmetry and cacophony, its medley of bitter ironies, broken promises, and isolated individuals, would seem to refute the aesthetic theory set forth above. Modernity itself — the world we see around us and the formative principles it suggests — seems to deny my claim of the integrity of life and art.

This situation derives from a number of causes. First, most art has long since ceased to be celebratory. The scientific revolution of the late Renaissance introduced a mechanistic view of nature, which focused attention on the material bases of phenomena and away from their significance as the embodiments of ideas. Mechanistic science thus constituted an attack not only on philosophy in general but on philosophical art (Platonic/Aristotelian mimesis).

This attack was compounded by the rise of Romanticism, a movement partly a revolt against materialism and reductivism of the scientific revolution, which was equally inimical to classic art. Intent on finding subject matter that was at once solidly real and impervious to mechanistic analysis, Romantics generally disregarded the notion of art as embodiment of idea and developed in its place the notion of art as expression of personal sentiment. With this change, art lost its ritual power to invoke universals and took on a demonic power to liberate emotions. By the same token, art exchanged its message of cultural communality for one of radical individualism, and its stabilizing influence for an ethic of revolution.

The surface of art changed more gradually. No longer imitation in the Aristotelian sense (because it no longer imitated ideas), Romantic art nonetheless was still representational: poetry sounded like song, classical music like dance, women in paintings were curved rather than pointed. But this representational residue was itself doomed. Representational art, though originally accepted as part of the Romantic agenda, ran counter to the individualism, experimentalism, and distrust of universals that were at the heart of the movement. Having no ideas to back it up, representation teetered uncomfortably for a few decades, an effigy without a subject.

By the turn of the twentieth century representational art in all genres was being replaced by various forms of expressionism. Poetry was losing its resemblance to song and moving toward its present resemblance to prose. Classical music was in the process of divorcing itself from song, dance, and (in important cases) natural harmonics. The visual arts were rejecting not only traditional ideas and figures but all resemblance to the customary experience of the senses. By midcentury most art had ceased, even in appearance, to celebrate life through an evocation of life's sensible dimensions.

Moreover, changing socioeconomic conditions have dramatically narrowed the scope of art. Gone are the great patrons whose courts supported whole artistic communities and ensured intimate communication between art and politics. Instead we have a vast art bazaar, a huge decentralized arena whose values are determined by experts and whose goods are hoarded by curators and collectors. Just beyond this bazaar is an even more extensive marketplace, a circus of mass media — pop music, television, movies — in which art is marketed as a "product" and beauty considered a form of packaging.

Serious artists, of course, still abound, but alienated from a unified social context, they abound as a class unto themselves, a group whose vision and technique evolve independently rather than interfacing with its culture. In a world of specialization, art, too, has become a specialty, not just as a separate discipline but as a cultural island on which artists, critics, and academicians exist more to please one another than to edify society. Socioeconomic evolution has changed art from an integral cultural function into an isolated elitist activity, from a political expression to an apolitical if not antipolitical statement.

These changes in ideology and market conditions have had inevitable effects on the quality of art. The Romantic mandate for self-expression, dutifully observed by generations of artists, long ago succeeded in exhausting the potentialities of Western individual "self" and is now condemned either to endless repetitions or evasive ironies. Nor would contemporary culture — at least "market" culture — appear to offer any worthwhile alternatives. In a society of technicians and entrepreneurs, of consumers protected equally from nuclear disaster and body odor, there is little room for tragic vision. In a society so permissive that it can neither praise virtue nor condemn vice, there

is little room for comic teaching. Liberal society offers art neither a solid basis for its own ideas nor a hard surface to push off
against. In terms of the ancient celebratory model, modern art
has neither goal nor subject.

What does all this imply about art and evolution? With the
start of this chapter in mind, we might argue that society, as it
has evolved beyond pain, has also evolved beyond art. The argument would run as follows: art was necessary as a social catalyst
so long as society fought hard for its own material sustenance
and lived in fear of environmental catastrophe. Now the fight
and the fear are gone. Progress has buried both so deep that
they seem never to have existed at all. With them are buried and
forgotten a miscellany of connected human traits, including re-
ligion, most forms of courage and chivalry, the urgent communality born of shared danger, and the impulse of art. The art
that remains, for all its fanfare and bravado, is a ghost, an after-
thought, an imitation of an imitation, or if none of the above, a
feeble effort to remind society of ancient anguish and greatness.

Is this situation permanent? In order to see any hope at all for
celebratory art, one must look outside art and into the social
context that supports it. Though fragmented and often confused, liberal society is no wasteland. One of its salient qualities
is pluralism, by which I mean not only entertaining a variety of
ideas but a bias toward the creation of new ones. Indeed, it
might be said that liberal democracy has adopted change as a
mechanism integral in its own survival, in the sense that it regularly appropriates ideas that seem to work and just as regularly
discards ideas that seem not to. Liberal society, as it were, has
bought into evolution and done very well in the bargain.

Given this evolutionary character, it is possible to imagine
that some form of celebratory art may reappear as a competitor
in the liberal arena. It may vie with other art forms as a medium
of expression and delight; in the curious justice of the marketplace, it may win itself a position. True, liberal pluralism is

plagued by its own reactionary tendencies; true, it is ill at ease with the universalism of classic celebratory art and with the "idealistic" philosophy that such art suggests. But liberal pluralism may take kindly to such principles as universalism and idealism if they are expressed not as philosophical manifestos but as artistic principles, and not as reminders of the past but as messages from the future.

More specifically, let us examine the materials for renewal that are at hand. It should be clear from the preceding chapters that creative thought in general partakes of many principles that traditionally have been applied to art. Creative thinkers in any field are open to inspiration; touched by beauty, they are lovers of form; they study and imitate nature. Given the parameters sketched above, such thinkers might even be called celebrators of life, but in their case the celebration is not an end (as it is with primitive and classic artists) but the by-product of another search. As such, the sense of celebration is personal rather than communal. Had innovators the desire to communicate it, they would have to indulge in art.

Can such a desire be reinstilled? Barring catastrophes, the feeling of shared jeopardy that inspired primitive art will be unavailable in the future. On the other hand, the spirit of classical art — the sense of imitation as a quest into the heart of ideas — remains an available option. The source of this option, surprisingly, is not in the arts or the humanities but rather in modern science. As I tried to show in Chapter 6, recurrent references to "beauty" across the sciences suggest a new interest in this abstract idea as a link between the disciplines. As a unifying abstraction, the sense of beauty may conceivably spread to the social sciences and beyond, unfolding new topics of discourse and an aesthetic dimension in fields previously considered value free.

Such a perspective could also generate new forms of art. It is likely that these new forms would constitute a radical departure from modernism (as well as from most of what is currently called postmodernism), and not impossible that they would appropriate, for their own distinct perspective, elements of the traditional aesthetic that modernism has renounced. Farfetched as this thought may seem, the progress of science, which once helped divorce art from the rest of culture, may become a means of reuniting the two.

19 *The Diplomacy of Invention*

And one ought to consider that there is nothing more difficult to pull off, more chancy to succeed in, or more dangerous to manage, than the introduction of a new order of
things.

— Niccolò Machiavelli, *The Prince*

AN IDEA can exist in a variety of forms. It can be a set of
thoughts in the mind of a single individual, an independent
concept not yet put down on paper, perhaps not yet even in
words. It can be on paper or some other physical medium, in
abstract or complete, but not yet published. It can be published
or broadcast or otherwise communicated to the world at large.
Using the word "idea" to describe each of these phenomena,
we sometimes miss important functional distinctions between
the nature of the thought at one stage and its nature at another.
In particular, we may miss the ways in which the process of expression and publication — what we might call the "socialization" of the idea — changes the idea itself.

This chapter will consider the key levels in the socialization
of innovative ideas. My aim is to outline problems characteristic of each stage and to suggest that each set of problems calls

not only for a reconsideration of the idea itself, but also for a special sort of statesmanship or "diplomacy" on the part of the innovator. In conclusion, I will focus on an apparent contradiction attaching to our notion of an "idea": the dichotomy between the sort of integrity associated with inventiveness and the diplomatic skills often required to get ideas accepted.

Suppose you are an independent mechanical engineer, young and unknown but with a formidable imagination and a high-class background in mechanics and chemistry. You have access to a facility that includes a drafting studio, a lab, and a machine shop. You have worked hard on your own projects for a number of years, suffering many failures but never doubting your ability to improve and prevail.

Then one morning, in the shower, a terrific idea strikes you. You conceive of an internal combustion engine that has only seven moving parts and runs on sea water. To design and build the thing will take some doing, but nothing beyond your proven ability.

Ultimate success with your water motor takes three quite separate types of expertise. The skills needed to conceptualize and draft the design for this machine are different in kind from the skills needed to build a working model or produce a complete salable product. Getting a good contract from Rolls-Royce or General Motors or forming your own company or fending off the petroleum interests and the trade unions would call for altogether different talents. Broadly speaking, these skills may be characterized as conceptual, technical, and interpersonal or political.

You might expect, since my subject here is "the diplomacy of invention," that I am interested only in the last of these three categories. But both the conceptual and technical levels of achievement have political implications of their own. *Conceptually,* you can come up with innovations which, though beneficial, are irrelevant to society's currently approved agenda. Conversely, you can develop ideas which, though implicitly harmful and destabilizing, are likely to be accepted because they promise immediate and easy gain. *Technically,* various embodiments of a single new idea can vary widely in initial appeal. You would not wish to present your water-burning engine with a noisy glasspack muffler belching black and briny foam; this would be like sculpting your life's masterpiece in bath soap or scoring your latest serious sonata for bagpipe and kazoo. Politics applies to every sort of thought for the simple reason that we do not have ideas for ourselves alone. Hence we have to consider the diplomacy of invention at the conceptual and technical levels as well as on the more explicitly political level.

THE CONCEPTUAL LEVEL:
THE PARABLE OF THE HOLE

The difference between new ideas and conventional thought is as elemental as that between fire and water. Innovative thought not only challenges the explicit beliefs of conventional institutions but questions the substructures that support these beliefs. Conventional thought, moreover, characteristically misinterprets innovation because the conventional idea of what is "new" has nothing to do with innovation at all. A story from the Italian Renaissance symbolically offers insight into these distinctions.

> You will not have forgotten the foolishness of that abbot . . . who was present one day when Duke Federico [da Montefeltro] was addressing what should be done with the great mass of earth which had been excavated for the foundations of this palace, which he was then building, and said: "My lord, I have an excellent idea where to put it. Give orders that a great pit be dug, and without further trouble it can be put into that." Duke Federico replied, not without laughter, "And where shall we put the earth that is excavated in digging this pit of yours?" Said the abbot: "Make it big enough to hold both."

The abbot's idea is ridiculous, but in subtle variations it is generally the way in which people in entrenched systems think about innovation. When they are faced with problems of any kind, their reflex is to dig their hole deeper or, by way of variety, to dig a new one. Digging may be expressed in the creation of a new office, a new committee, or an additional form; on the national scale, not only these remedies but new commissions, laws, and taxes are very much in style. The diggers' rationale is based on the assumption that the world cannot be reorganized or reassessed, but can only be added on to, an assumption that applies not only to problem solving but to the birth of ideas in general. The conventional view of progress, in other words, is *elaborative:* what the conventional mind sees as "new" is generally no more than an elaboration on the pattern of the status quo.

Understanding this attitude and its bases helps answer a couple of troublesome questions. First, we can now see why most of the thousands of things commonly advertised as new departures — women's fashions, intellectual vogues, cars, novels, painkillers, and election platforms — have little real impact on history and are either remaindered or totally forgotten by the next turn of the cycle. Conventional "newness," mere elaboration on accepted principles, can never carry the force of real change. Instead, elaboration is at root a force of stability, a kind of balancing mechanism.

Second, we can see why institutions and the institutional mentality so frequently shun real innovation. Real innovation, which characteristically demands the revision of whole structures and the rethinking of basic principles, does not fit the conventional idea of newness; instead it looks awkward, unbalanced, outlandish. Innovative ideas are shunned not so much because they "look new" as because they do not conform to the common assumption that elaboration is newness.

Of course this does not mean that institutions carry on unchanged; it does mean, however, that the process of change is somewhat more complicated than young innovators might hope. Some change occurs because of planning, some because of crisis. Sometimes a huge structure of elaborations, grown top-heavy, unbalanced by externally induced trends, tilts slowly to one side like a bay tree and establishes a new center of gravity. And sometimes institutions listen to new ideas. Innovators must become acquainted with the rich and frustrating network of processes. They must accept the fact that no show of benevolence or proof of genius will ever wholly defuse the shock of a new thought. Without suppressing or corrupting their own thought, they must learn to understand, in addition, the way others think.

On the conceptual level, then, innovators should review their new ideas in terms of the social good or harm that these ideas may produce. Moreover they should, so to speak, bend their minds to reassess their own ideas from *outside:* from the surprised perspective of people who have been accustomed to the old. Understanding the outside perspective may enable innovators to express their ideas effectively.

THE TECHNICAL LEVEL: THE PARABLE OF THE WHITE SUIT

Because they suggest a reworking of basic principles, most original ideas are capable of a variety of different embodiments. Your brine-burning engine, for example, can be introduced as an elegant miniature or a 3,000-horsepower turbine; it can be presented running a generator, a hydraulic system, or a speedboat. The embodiment in which an idea is submitted for approval — as suggesting relatively broad or narrow ranges of use and creating a relatively great or small degree of shock — is an important element in the diplomacy of invention.

The Man in the White Suit, a motion picture that speaks profoundly about innovation and society, tells the story of a young chemist (Alec Guinness) who invents an apparently indestructible synthetic fabric. He greets society (here represented by manufacturers and the workers' trade union) with the glad tidings that the world's garment worries are over; as a sample, he models a white suit. Society's response is less than ecstatic, combining, in effect, the more passionate elements of the Chartist uprising with the general thrust of the Spanish Inquisition. The manufacturers persecute the chemist for threatening their sales, the unionists for threatening their jobs. He escapes martyrdom only because his compound proves to be unstable and his suit falls to pieces.

The Man in the White Suit presents two archetypal crises in the diplomacy of invention. First, industrialists and unionists alike reject the chemist's invention because they are unable to conceive of the vast possibilities for profit and work that it will open up. Caught in the networks of an elaborative system, they rebel against an idea that would make them change their configurations and ways of thinking. Second, the initial "embodiment" of the idea as a white suit (with implications both utopian and messianic) is overly aggressive and rather naive. A diplomatic inventor would have insisted on something less blatant, like brake linings or military underwear. The technical diplomacy of invention, in other words, is based on the recognition that new ideas are naturally threatening to dwellers on the affected turf, and that small but secure beachheads are in this case superior to all-or-nothing assaults.

Two episodes from the life of the inventor Cornelis Drebbel illustrate the dangers of "undiplomatic" presentation. Drebbel, who had mastered the principles of solar heating, could have offered his ideas to his government in a variety of feasible and economical forms. Instead he chose the most ambitious form possible, an almost utopian urban-scale project that would have cost millions. In framing the project this way, Drebbel made two major errors in diplomacy. First, he proposed a huge drain on the resources of a royal family who were famous for their money troubles. Second, without first suggesting a small-scale demonstration, he asked for this monster sum to be risked on a scheme so technically advanced as to seem, to most laymen, quite fanciful.

Another of Drebbel's presentations was even more disastrous. Precociously skilled in the chemistry of artificial refrigeration, Drebbel invited King James I and some courtiers into a room and made the air grow suddenly cold. Drebbel's audience, the king included, jumped to their feet and exited at top speed. An innovation that might have earned wonderment and support produced terror.

Drebbel's experiences give insight into the human nature of innovation. They show us the fear and disbelief that typically greet new discoveries, as well as the excessive enthusiasm and bravado that can ruin an innovator's effect on society. They suggest to us that the first embodiment of a new idea be relatively modest, that it appear as part of an unambitious but indisputably helpful suggestion. It is better that a true birth of imagination first meet the world with the manners expected of a well-instructed child.

THE MORALITY OF SELF-PROMOTION

Innovators should determine their means of promoting their own work, discussing it, or evaluating the work of others, in the light of the conditions outlined above. They must remember that they lead a kind of dual existence: as independent hunters for new truth and as very human members of a culture whose bywords are prosperity and stability. Awareness of this duality can cushion the shock of rejection and increase the possibility of success.

Practical strategies. Certain political strategies have proved effective in the presentation and protection of new ideas. To some people (and not always the best of people), these modalities seem to come naturally. Others of us have to learn them. I offer these strategies as a list of suggestions, without much further comment.

- Discuss new initiatives in terms of their positive potential rather than beginning with negative criticisms of the status quo. Adopt the rhetorical posture of one who gives, not of one who petitions, questions, or asserts.
- Discuss your idea privately, as much as possible, with individual members of the group who must decide on it. Listen carefully to their suggestions; implement and acknowledge any that are helpful.
- Of all components of rhetoric, none is more popular (or more frequently misused) than data. Be ready not only to use data in support of your thesis but in answer to data-supported criticisms by others.
- Don't feel that you always have to respond substantively to negative criticism. Negative thought has little independent sustaining structure and is soon forgotten. A brilliant rebuttal to criticism is often less effective than a courteous acknowledgment or an inspired silence.
- New catchwords or phrases are often useful in the presentation of ideas, but only when they are firmly based in familiar structures of discourse. Most effective in this regard are variations on the nascent clichés that still convey a sense of newness to most listeners. Innovation sometimes disguises itself as elaboration.
- True innovation is both novel and humane. Therefore you should be able to support some aspects of your proposal with

the rhetoric of originality, others with the rhetoric of consensus.

- Share or forgo the credit for your ideas as often as possible. They will go further that way, and faster.
- Every subject, no matter how important, has a funny side. Don't ignore humor in presenting your idea or defending it, in dealing with rejection or success.
- Remember that defeated proposals are soon forgotten and can soon be resubmitted, especially if they are couched in somewhat different terms. Ideas that meet with total apathy or disapproval at first can succeed brilliantly when reproposed a few years down the line. You have to be tough enough to endure the first shot, patient enough to let things rest for a while, and confident enough to take the risk a second or third time.

These strategies, as I have said, can be used by well-meaning and ill-meaning people alike. It is at least as important to recognize such methods in the hands of others as to be able to use them yourself. They are weapons of practical power that can be called into the service of conscience; it would therefore be well to remember that the code that has best reconciled conscience with practical power is the code of chivalry.

This brings us to the moral issue raised by the role of "diplomacy" in innovation: Is it ethically degrading to try to sell one's own ideas in the marketplace? Experience and common sense would seem to argue yes. Shakespeare himself bewailed having (as an actor) clowned around in front of audiences, "a motley to the view." Special forms of embarrassment attach to simplifying one's own ideas and promoting one's own interests publicly.

But instead of bewailing the impurity of public promotions, innovators might better question the purity of their private motives. Innovation is necessarily an aggressive act, not only because it enlarges human liberty and power, but also because it is the product of a bold individual assertion, a new word breaking the silence of history. To this extent, innovators who seek to promote their ideas in the marketplace are not corrupting the impulse of invention but are extending an aggressive impulse toward its natural goal. Aggressive action in the marketplace is the objective correlative of the aggressive imagination. Self-promotion is sometimes the only means by which valid ideas can obtain a hearing. Self-promotion can open up the creative psychology in new ways. Though he bewailed his public displays, Shakespeare realized that "these blenches gave my heart another youth."

And the marketplace, as a potential habitat for creative people, has often been underrated. It has different rules, a different language, but it is no less human, colorful, or potentially fruitful than the world of ideas. In its own way the marketplace is amenable to creativity and innovation and even holds, as its quite exclusive property, the possibility that contribution will be rewarded by trust and love. The artful strategies listed above become in this light something more than strategies: they may be seen as suggesting a "poetics" of statesmanship, a framework of styles and topics that can itself become a source of innovation.

The moral accusations against self-promotion can be turned back upon themselves. What can we say of those innovators who are most studiously protected from market pressures, the natural scientists? These innovators are usually paid to have ideas by corporations or else do grant-supported research in their laboratories on university campuses. Aside from preparing periodic grant applications, they do not have to "sell" their ideas. Scientists do not have to worry about the reception of their ideas, because the great program they contribute to — the advancement of human knowledge and power — has society's almost unanimous support. They do not have to worry about the potential misuse of their ideas or about their underlying historical significance, because such "specialties" as ethics and history lie outside their fields. They are encouraged to believe that their research is "pure," that is, uncorrupted by interest.

But from a political point of view, modern scientific research is not free at all. Its direction is largely determined by the interests of the institutions that fund research grants and, more generally, by the priorities of society at large. Our ethical judgment of natural scientists depends primarily on whether or not we unequivocally endorse these interests. If we do, we may confidently praise scientists as heroes of progress; if we do not, we may criticize them, in the main, as moral escapists who allow private and public interests to milk them like aphids. Scientists' freedom from the marketplace can be, conversely, an alienation from responsibility.

We may conclude then that, though demanding and often frustrating, the diplomacy of invention is a necessary art and a respectable one. Innovators who reject it deny their own social role. Innovators who are protected from it tend to be morally stunted. Innovators who despise it, but pay middlemen to practice it in their behalf, are hypocrites. Like all political arts, it is subject to misuse, but at its best it can be a medium of learning and an implement of justice.

20 The Eyes of Laughter

Groucho Marx to the humorist S. J. Perelman, on receiving a copy of Perelman's new book, *Dawn Ginsbergh's Revenge*: "From the moment I picked up your book until I laid it down, I was convulsed with laughter. Someday I intend reading it."

THE HUMOROUS may be described either as a way of looking at the world or as a visible dimension of the world as observed. What sort of world does humor see, and what does its way of seeing have to do with creative thought? To these questions I will suggest the following answers: that humor looks at the world of human liberty, that its specific subject is the finiteness or limit of liberty, that in circumscribing our freedom it offers freedom of a better sort, and that it is an important creative form because it conveys profound teaching through such media as analysis and discovery.

Humor, to begin with, observes limits of its own with striking precision. It seldom intrudes into scientific or technical journals, into instruction manuals, into library card catalogues or other receptacles of data. Scientists, technicians, and librarians may well crack jokes about their work, but they do not encounter the funny as a necessary part of it. On the other hand, counselors, artists, teachers, leaders, and people who study human affairs in order to speak or write about them almost invariably perceive a comic spirit at work in the heart of what they do. This comic spirit is seldom dominant or even aggressive; rather it seems complementary to the genuinely serious aspects of their work. Humor, in other words, is inappropriate to the study of nature, to the advance of technology, to the accumulation of data. Conversely, it seems not only appropriate but necessary in the conduct and scrutiny of human affairs.

This distinction may seem simple, but simple distinctions are not always barren of mystery. Why should humor reside in certain pursuits and be absent from others? Why should a traveling salesman or a baseball nickname or a bishop's hobby be humorous while a DNA molecule and a computer and a bibliography are not? Because, I think, the latter subjects belong to systems closed to the exercise of freedom, while the former belong to systems open to it. A humorous potential is inherent in all phenomena that suggest choice or value.

Almost everything that's funny involves some kind of choice. We laugh about mischievous choices, wrong choices, choices hardened into mechanistic habits, failures to choose when choice is required. We laugh when external circumstance (coincidence, education, misinformation) or internal circumstance (passion, instinct) misdirects choice in certain ways. From these examples it is apparent that humor looks at freedom very specifically: it examines the limits of freedom, the line between what we choose and what is otherwise determined. You might say that humor is a critique of freedom, that it etches in part, against the solid background of nature, the bright but slender profile of liberty.

In performing this function, humor has powerful assistance from the art form tragedy. Like the subjects of humor or comedy, the subjects of tragedy are the expression and limitation of freedom, but tragedy examines these subjects more intensely and on a larger scale. Tragic figures are much freer than comic figures. Tragic figures do not trip over tables or don transsexual disguises. Liberated from foible and minor circumstance, tragedy can explore the broader boundaries of freedom, which include heroism, loneliness, terror, agony, and death. Tragedy, in effect, completes the profile of liberty begun by comedy; thus finished, the profile may be seen as a cameo of human liberty at large.

But words like "limit" and "critique," though accurate in themselves, fall short of conveying the full effect of the humorous or the tragic. The limits of freedom cannot be conceived accurately unless freedom has had full scope within them; a critique is injudicious unless it includes a positive appreciation. What separates real humor from mere derision is that humor retains, along with its criticism, a spirit of sympathy; we cannot laugh except at a human reality that we implicitly share. More broadly, comedy and tragedy operate by evoking within us the very impulses of liberty that they ultimately limit, enabling us to experience, in turn, those impulses, the shock of restriction and the sense of reconciliation with a larger social or natural order. This is the long-appreciated cathartic function of comic and tragic art. Comic endings may be happy and tragic sad, but as the product of an expression-restriction-reconciliation development, they are generically similar.

VISION AND THE CHEMISTRY OF LAUGHTER

The quality of comic and tragic vision has been the subject of many excellent studies; more pertinent to my interests here is the homely phenomenon of laughter itself. What makes us laugh, and what does the experience of laughter entail? Let us leave aside such special forms of humor as caricature and pun (at which we seldom genuinely laugh), and concentrate on the locus classicus of laughter, the anecdote. Unlike caricature and pun, anecdote depends for its laughter on development in time, and thus it can be more readily anatomized. Of the two anecdotes that follow, the first will be familiar from the preceding chapter and the second from the start of this one.

You will not have forgotten the foolishness of that abbot . . . who was present one day when Duke Federico [da Montefeltro] was addressing what should be done with the great mass of earth which had been excavated for the foundations of this palace, which he was then building, and said: "My lord, I have an excellent idea where to put it. Give orders that a great pit be dug, and without further trouble it can be put into that." Duke Federico replied, not without laughter, "And where shall we put the earth that is excavated in digging this pit of yours?" Said the abbot: "Make it big enough to hold both."

When the humorist S. J. Perelman had finished writing his early *Dawn Ginsbergh's Revenge,* he sent a copy to his friend Groucho Marx. Marx responded in a note: "From the moment I picked up your book until I laid it down, I was convulsed with laughter. Someday I intend reading it."

Different from each other in every detail, these stories nonetheless observe the same classic phenomenology of laughter. Each of them — and indeed almost every good anecdote or gag — begins by assuming an atmosphere of human freedom or effectiveness or dignity: an elder submitting a constructive proposal to his duke and a young author sharing his latest work with a respected friend. Into this conventional situation a single anomaly is introduced: an attack on reason, so severe as to subvert not only the normalcy of the situation but also, temporarily, the very sanity of the world in which the situation exists. In good anecdotes this subversion is so successful that, in its wake, even totally reasonable statements are impossible to take seriously.

What does our laughter at such stories release? Precisely those tensions — anxieties, efforts, embarrassment — necessitated by our presence in a conventional and allegedly reasonable world. Humor in this way is a homeopathic cure, liberating us from our own illusions of freedom, dignity, and power, medicating our suppressed feelings of psychological disorder with a creative disorder of its own.

But more than symptomatic relief is involved here. By ushering us into a world whose dynamics subverts reason and propriety, humor suggests that reason and propriety cannot be accepted as the sole arbiters of experience. People skilled in the art of laughter are by that token liberated from the provincialism of the single mind. Implicit in that liberation is freedom from the sanctimonious self, the earnest and defensive ego that is the by-product of prolonged participation in adult life. The homeopathy of laughter is metaphysical as well as medical. In laughing at the limitations of our freedom, we meet with a more remarkable liberty, born of vision and cognate with self-knowledge.

That such laughter can have permanent positive effects is evidenced by a story once told me by a friend. Quite early in his career he had become head of a small division in a stock brokerage. No sooner was he in office than he hatched an ambitious plan to reorganize his division. After much scribbling and revising he typed out an elaborate proposal, supporting it with about fifty pages of data and projections.

It occurred to this young executive that, before submitting the proposal to his boss, he should get an expert reading. He then had a gem of an idea. A similar reorganization, on an immeasurably grander scale, had just been masterminded by a bank president who also happened to be the most famous man on Wall Street. By sending the proposal to this great man, my friend might get some good advice, receive an endorsement that would help him gain easier acceptance for his plan, and strike up a friendship with someone he greatly respected.

The trouble was, he had never met the man. Eloquence was in order. He wrote a lengthy letter, detailing his background, outlining corporate history, acknowledging the bank president's expertise, and requesting the man's guidance. In style he strove to be dignified without vanity, informal without familiarity. He stuffed letter and papers into a manila envelope and addressed it. Bypassing his secretary (why leave any room for error?) he went downstairs and dropped the packet in a mailbox.

At his desk the next day, my friend noticed with some shock that his typed proposal, complete with all supporting material but without the covering letter, was still on his desk. How very embarrassing, he thought, and jumped up to get another manila envelope. But he stopped halfway down the hall, feeling suddenly cold and weak. If he hadn't mailed the proposal with his letter, why had the envelope been so heavy when he carried it to the mailbox? Why had it made such a satisfying thump after being pushed past the metal door? Clearly he had stuffed something rather big into the envelope, and this thing, whatever it was, was now speeding irrevocably on its way, advertised as a brilliant new reorganization proposal.

He went back and searched his desk top. Identifying an object by its absence was frustratingly harder than recognizing an object unexpectedly found there. He would have to write the man another letter. But as he reached for paper, the nature and stupefying extent of his error was suddenly clear. There was no blank paper on his desk. About fifty pages of unused office letterhead had disappeared.

A strange queasiness came over my friend, the sort of feeling he might have had if his elevator had abruptly started to move sideways or his cab, stopped at a traffic light in the rain, had begun to sink deeper and deeper into a puddle.

Then he began to feel chagrin. Like some nasty tropical

worm, it screwed itself deeper into him with each motion of body and turn of mind. He felt the shame of a child caught stealing candy. He felt naked, puny, and befouled.

But as he drove home that evening, he suddenly began to laugh. He would laugh uncontrollably, no matter where he was, whenever the memory returned to him for the next week; years later, he still cannot think about this experience with a straight face. He told me that this silly incident, and two or three others like it, taught him how to look at his own career and that he remembers it invariably during solemn and dignified professional rituals.

LAUGHTER AS CONTINUUM

I have suggested that laughter seems to usher us into another world. The experience of the young executive is similar to the first two anecdotes in that each takes us momentarily (to use Lewis Carroll's wonderful phrase) "through the looking-glass," momentarily out of the assumed cycle of cause and effect and into a weirdly reversed perspective. It might be said that this perspective is present in all humor, but it is perhaps more accurate to say that the strange place is always there, somewhere inside us, and that everything that appeals to it in the proper way has to be funny. Laughter may be relief, therapy, and enlightenment, but it is all these things solely because it is a return to a mental place that we know intimately but tend to forget about, a haven devoted to the subjects of childhood and the birth of dreams. In this sense, to laugh is to go home, to overcome for a moment the alienation and secrecy of being grown up.

LAUGHTER AS ANALYSIS

Describing a similar world at the beginning of Chapter 10, I speculated that inventive people possessed a special entrée to it. Certainly, an individual's expertise in the art of laughter suggests the integrity and self-awareness connected repeatedly with inventiveness. But it would be wrong to romanticize laughter as being exclusively an excursion into the unconscious or the province of misrule. Though many people may be funny on impulse, great comedians (Geoffrey Chaucer, for example, and Charles Dickens) employ humor analytically as part of an exploration of human nature. To such humorists, the creation of laughter involves the elaboration of seemingly reasonable and normal situations that are subverted by unexpected analogy or anomaly. These developments put reader or listener into a momentary state of confusion that is resolved by the "discovery" of laughter (see Chapter 3). And this discovery brings with it, momentarily, a rediscovery of self, a glimpse of human continuity.

As an effective and easily available mode of analysis, humor carries with it two other elements that make it a valuable exercise in creativity. First, by playing off normal or conventional situations, it requires that we recognize and appreciate "form" — here the accepted forms of social intercourse and the elements of our conventional self-image. When we do, humor educates us in awareness and independence. Second, by forcing us to recognize strange analogies or anomalies in the forms we see, humor encourages us to conceive of new forms, grotesque but uniquely illuminating. The abbot's suggestion of bigger and bigger holes, the thought of Groucho laughing at an unopened book, and the absurdist image of the blank proposal symbolically convey truths about the limits of human freedom that might have been impossible to express in any other way.

So helpful are these experiences, and so many the other virtues of laughter, that one might extol it as the ultimate form of vision, the only vision capable of including and illuminating all aspects of life. One might try to build a whole life on humor, employing it (as the ancients used wine) as a global tonic. But the very power of humor is also its limitation. Its magic is dissolved by the laughter that is its proper goal; having laughed, we sense for an instant the wistfulness of dreamers returned to toil. Like many other art forms, humor is a seasonal celebration, a vision limited by time.

HUMOR AND INNOVATION

Because inventions, innovations, and independent thought in general are acts of liberty, they are highly vulnerable to humor. The victims of humor may be the innovators themselves, either when (as with the abbot or the young executive) their inventions misfire, or when (as with Perelman) their aspirations are cleverly deflated by a critic. Innovation always appears as a temporary distortion of form, and as such is particularly amenable to the jest.

Innovators are often derided, sometimes quite bitterly, by representatives of the vested interests whose territory they seem to threaten. This "humor of reaction" is not only a practical weapon but also a cathartic means of relieving its wielders' anxiety and resentment. It operates in every arena from the children's playground to advanced scientific debates. Its locus classicus is Genesis, 37:19, where Joseph's brethren remark in jest, "Behold, this dreamer cometh."

But the perspective may be reversed. In providing new liberty, all valid innovation suggests the limitations of past liberty, thus carrying in itself the potential for humorously turning the tables on its deriders. Humor is friend to innovators, moreover, because in its subversion of the customary and the predictable, it is analogous to what they most seriously do. Great inspirations are not totally unlike great jokes, and we should pause in thought before drawing a heavy line of demarcation between the great historical advances of intellect and the pranks of youngsters. Major innovators and reformers from Socrates to Winston Churchill have been blessed with the eyes of laughter, a power that functioned not only as a relief from, but as a symbolic expression of, their urgent calling.

21 *Ideology and*
Moral Philology

But the Idols of the Market Place are the most troublesome
of all — idols which have crept into the understanding
through the alliances of words and names. For men believe
that their reason governs words, but it is also true that words
react on the understanding, and this it is that has rendered
philosophy and the sciences sophistical and inactive.

— Francis Bacon, *Novum Organum*

Nothing so needs reforming as other people's habits.

— Mark Twain, *Pudd'nhead Wilson*

WHAT DO I mean by "ideology"? Let me begin by looking at
two ways of comparing human beings with apes.

Traditional satire (for example, *Gulliver's Travels*) dwelt on
similarities between human beings and apes as means of illus-
trating the chronic limitations of human nature. The ape's be-
havioral patterns, its grooming, its play, its mating, its social interactions, were exploited by satirists as a destructive mimicry
of similar mechanisms in humanity. This satire is based on a
world view deeply skeptical of human virtue and highly critical
of human pretensions to progress and excellence.

Modern science, on the other hand, characteristically sees the same ape/human similarities as proof of the remarkable intelligence of apes. (After all, if they're so like us, they've got to be bright!) This opinion is based on a world view deeply rooted in the idea of progress and the sense of human excellence.

To understand the difference between the classical view and our own is to begin to appreciate the power of ideology. It is also to exercise one of the important talents that human beings have and apes do not: the faculty of self-examination.

Ideology is at once the matrix from which creativity is born and the barrier against which it strains. As a pattern of ideas absorbed by us as children from our society, ideology gives each of us intellectual viability among our fellows and introduces us to a variety of important issues. But as an essentially unphilosophical system, born of social necessity, governed by historical circumstance, incomplete, arbitrary, and insidiously tyrannical, ideology is unfriendly to independent thought. Creativity has no choice but to grow in ideology, no goal except to move beyond it.

The conflict between ideology and creativity may be illustrated by comparing ideology with philosophy. Let us say that both philosophy and ideology are systems of ideas on which people base their judgments and actions. Philosophy is an open system. Its premises are clear, and it retains, in addition to these premises, a method by which they may be reexamined.

Ideology, on the other hand, is a closed system whose premises, whether explicit or implicit, are unavailable to scrutiny. Ideology causes us to judge and to act automatically, uninquisitively. We do not question our own judgments or actions and have not the means of questioning them if we wanted to. When others question them, we fall back to generalizations which, though we have not examined them, we accept as unimpeachable; we use these generalizations to displace responsibility for error from ourselves to our questioners. While philosophy evolves, more often than not, by recognizing its own excesses or failings, ideology can never see itself as "wrong." When it evolves at all, ideology evolves unconsciously, not through distinct reforms of self-awareness but through slow, unconscious cultural realignments.

These factors can make ideology a vehicle for laziness and self-deceit. Ideology enables us to pass judgments on a variety of issues while lacking adequate information or analytic skill or commitment to discovering the truth. And ideology not only substitutes for information, analysis, and commitment, but also for conscience. The fact that a given action or lack of action conforms to our ideology absolves us from having to worry about it or take responsibility for it. With ideology we may appear to be well informed, analytically skillful, inquisitive, conscientious, and morally responsible without really being so.

This does not mean, of course, that ideologies are universally debilitating, or that they are all equally so. Some ideologies (for example, liberalism) actually have values such as inquiry and enlightenment built into them, while in others such values are prohibited. What it does mean is that a system is ideological to the extent that its values are assumed and unexamined, and that even edifying words like "enlightenment," if thus assumed and unexamined, can lose much of their positive force and function instead as false counters, near-empty clichés, or instruments of reaction. In this respect ideology is a kind of moral computer program, which is excellent at arranging information, providing precedents, expediting connections, and suggesting conclusions, but which cannot analyze its own structure or consciously evolve from it.

Recognizing the operation of ideology in others is a minor matter compared to locating it in ourselves and our peers. Ideology lies deep and is well protected. The mechanisms with which people defend ideology are precisely those with which they defend their personal integrity. For this very reason, the identification and analysis of one's own ideology are critical steps in the progress toward self-knowledge. Later in this chapter I will suggest a method by which these steps may be taken. A more suitable beginning, however, may be found in an examination of what may be called microideologies — modal or periodic value systems that we adopt or put aside as occasion warrants.

Microideology describes our behavior and sense of identity as they change in response to typical personal interactions: with our parents or our children, with friends, colleagues, or strangers, with our own or the opposite sex. These changes occur painlessly, often unconsciously, but they can be so profound as to activate, within the same individual, strikingly different presentations of character. To understand these expressions and their roots in circumstance is to understand, in little, a key factor of ideology. A homely enough set of such systems operates the way people generally behave in street traffic.

As pedestrians we are midgets in a giant world. We are deeply aware of our own physical weakness, in terms of limited speed and energy; we sense that we would not fare well in collisions with cars or bicycles. We view these potential antagonists with distaste and fear. Car drivers, faceless in their instruments of power and pollution, are potential homicides, sinister agents of a callous system. Bicyclists are mere outlaws, debased cowboys who combine the unbridled ambitions of the tyrant with the furtive quickness of the sneak. Conscious of the superior power of car drivers and bicyclists, we are ardent democrats and great believers in the law. Our Constitution, a great text written in stop signs, traffic lights, and speed limits, is defended with zeal and indignation, and nothing is quite so righteously satisfying as the knowledge that, by stepping into a pedestrian crossing at the right time, we have caused a car to stop.

As bicyclists we are strong advocates of the conservation of energy. Stop signs — the restrictive machinery of a callous system — pedestrians, and cars have importance to us less as independent moral entities than as obstacles that threaten us with the unthinkable toil of having to stop our bikes and pedal them back up to speed. As such, stodgy pedestrians and obscene cars are figures of reaction and oppression. They lack our spirit of adventure; they breed in the staleness of closed systems. Aware of our own maverick status, we feel entitled to use our wits. The bicyclian politics, which springs from a profoundly liberal commitment to the sharing of other people's rights, is seen to apply without discrimination on road, sidewalk, and lawn.

As car drivers we are important people in a hurry. Because we need not worry about our own vulnerability or energy, our main concern is time. We deplore the unreasonable regulations — born of a callous system — that delay our swift procedure from place to place, but more bitterly we resent the assorted rabble, some on foot and some on two-wheeled toys, who flaunt ill-bestowed liberty by milling around in the street. These loiterers and guerrillas are small, weak, and probably poor; they have no strength except in number; in spite of this they get ridiculously upset when someone fails to notice them. Doubtless sprung from the god of war, we are so imbued with epic high spirits that often we cannot tolerate even our own kind.

Though they may be somewhat exaggerated, the preceding examples suggest that generic value shifts characterize our normal daily journeys from task to task. I am concerned here less with the marvelous swiftness of these transformations than with the nature of the value systems involved. These value systems share a number of characteristics.

- First, each system is shared by all or almost all members of the class or set.
- Second, each is based on a subjective and limited understanding of the total situation (in this case, traffic).
- Third, each system has little regard for its own internal consistency or significance in context.
- Fourth, in each system ethical standards develop not out of

inquiry but directly out of the necessities of the particular situation.
• Fifth, these standards are not merely accepted but asserted sanctimoniously and defensively against members of other sets.

A sixth characteristic, implicit in all three examples, is perhaps most illuminating of all: the value systems of walker, biker, and driver, confusing and contradictory as they are, seem actually to assist them in carrying out the specific tasks they address. They allay doubt; they tranquilize anxiety; they rationalize aggressiveness; they dispel responsibility. As support systems and protective shells, they aid us in navigating through the complex channels of modern life. Much more comfortably than philosophy, ideology makes practical sense of the world. It assures us that experience has coherence and can be explained. It gives us confidence in ourselves as participants in a meaningful project.

To discuss the "limitations" of ideology is to discuss only half the problem. As important as the things we cannot do with ideology is the fact that we cannot do without it.

Such, in microcosm, is the nature of ideology. With one major exception, the same principles that apply to walkers, bicyclists, and drivers apply to liberals and conservatives, to Marxists, Freudians, feminists, and fundamentalists. The exception is that these latter ideologies, these supersystems, do not change when we get on or off a bicycle or in or out of a car. They are wedged firmly into our identity because they spring, rather than from temporary requirements, from the historical necessities of a whole nation, social class, or intellectual movement, and because they address, rather than some temporary role, our general condition as individuals in society.

A particular misunderstanding of ideology is characteristic of the young. Younger generations who reject established values generally have no idea that their own revolutionary programs will harden into protective ideologies. Moreover, they reject elements of systems without inquiring into the bases of systems. The hippies, for example, rebelled against the capitalism and conservatism of their parents while unconsciously retaining the materialism and anti-intellectualism on which those elements were based. This mistake left the hippies not only with empty heads but with hungry bellies; the upshot was a counterrevolution (the yuppies) which, with all the joy of new discovery, reinstated the old order. Thus revolution, by surprise, becomes a force of continuity, and generations, like tourists lost in a strange city, find themselves returning by various alleyways to the same square.

It is not enough simply to isolate and denounce ideology. To gain at least partial freedom from it, we must first make peace with it; we must understand its inevitable prevalence in others and our own vulnerability to it. The liberal arts afford various ways of meeting this challenge. Cultural history, as applied by many scholars, offers insights into the phenomenon of ideology by examining various ideologies of the past. Such insights are particularly informative when they apply to our own political and cultural background. Philosophy, anthropology, sociology, psychology, economics, and political science have all sponsored examinations of the substrata that lie beneath generally accepted ideas.

Perhaps more helpful than any of these, curiously enough, is the study of literature. Though they never bothered to invent the word, great satirists like Chaucer and Swift were profound students of ideology, as were major novelists like Hawthorne, Flaubert, Tolstoy, James, and Conrad. One of the primary functions of good fiction and drama is to establish a limited point of view — quite often one which is unquestioningly accepted by large elements of the author's own society — and play off against it ironically. Understanding literature properly, we may learn to recognize as such the oversights and contradictions that attend on our own points of view.

But none of these studies addresses the whole. None persistently explores those areas which might be called the heart of ideology: the premises of our view so profound as to be unspoken, the topics so long neglected as to be forgotten. For people to explore these idiosyncracies in their own ideology is almost as unlikely as it is for them to see through the backs of their own heads. One method, however, offers some hope of progress. To address it, we must return again to the distinction between philosophy and ideology.

I called philosophy an "open" system and spoke of it as combining a structure of ideas with an instrument of self-scrutiny. Philosophy, as defined above, is not purely conceptual: it is rather an interplay of concept and method. In this relation, method does not merely "apply" concepts: it studies and tests and reforms them, overseeing them the way a cat oversees her kittens. Because of this interplay, concepts (words or groups of words) are continuously reviewed, reassessed, and subjected to hypothetical variations.

Ideology, on the other hand, seems to be preeminently conceptual. Though given ideologies (for example, Marxism, feminism) may have built-in methods, the methods are not employed in self-analysis but exist as a way of criticizing other ideologies and globally asserting their own root concepts. How are these concepts structured? With Chapters 10 and 11 in mind, we may see them as radiating out from a series of key words, comprising the ideas and feelings that these words evoke and the relations between one set of words, ideas, and feelings and another.

Take, for example, the final words of the American Pledge of Allegiance: "with liberty and justice for all." The ideologue in me still feels a glow of pleasure at hearing these words. Yet history can point to no relationship as dynamically insecure as that between liberty and justice. Full-blooded ideologues do not analyze such interactions. By definition, ideologues analyze nothing that relates to their ideology. Instead they rely on the power commanded by the key word, either as support for a position of their own or as a bludgeon against a position held by someone else.

It follows, then, that ideology may be approached through a study of words, which might be called moral philology. It would analyze key words in an effort to establish the parent concepts they evoke. It would assemble and correlate, appreciate and criticize, the set of parent concepts suggested by groups of key words. Specifically, this study would ask the following questions about key words:

Does a given word suggest a single concept, or more than one?
If more than one, what do the concepts suggested have in common?
If more than one, do the concepts suggested contradict one another, and if so, how?
What do we intend when we use the key word?
Is our intention satisfied by the parent concept or concepts?
If not, how?
Are the constructs suggested by groups of key words harmonious or self-contradictory?

This sort of analysis is illustrated in Chapters 4, 8, 11, and 12 of this book, which suggest that the concepts evoked respectively by "analysis," "integrity," "self," and "freedom" are flawed and cannot, as now used, satisfactorily express the speaker's intention (also see Chapter 22, "modern"). Each chapter takes the additional step of showing how the word in question might be rehabilitated so as to evoke a reasonable concept effectively and without self-contradiction.

Such a study is far from new. It was an important part of the Socratic method of inquiry (dialectic) as evidenced in Platonic dialogues like the *Euthyphro,* the *Symposium,* and the *Republic.* In these dialogues Socrates takes three key words ("piety," "love," and "justice," respectively), pins down the concepts that they evoke, and subjects them to scrutiny. Socrates took a good deal of heat for his dogged adherence to this method, and more than anything else it may have been the cause of his condemnation and death. But society's violent response to moral philology is a testament to the potentially revolutionary power of this method.

Because of its perennial relevance, moral philology has never wholly disappeared from the rolls, but neither has it ever achieved much currency as a teaching method and a means of self-examination. It is a difficult study and (on the surface) a rather dry one. But it is perhaps unchallenged in exploring the ways of ideology and in devising means of escape from fixed channels. Whatever its limitations, moral philology has the unique advantage of beginning with an analysis of those very constructs which are to be the basis of all its later judgments. To do this is to avoid the self-defeating habit (typical of many other analytic approaches) of using these very key words, without examination, as the bases for further exploration and analysis.

The reassessment of key words is perhaps the most accessible and effective method of self-scrutiny available to us. And self-scrutiny, whether individual or cultural, is an important medium for innovation and a prerequisite for renewal.

22 The Ideology of Present Time

> It is not permitted to the most equitable of men to be a judge in his own cause.
>
> — Blaise Pascal, *Pensées*

LEO TOLSTOY's tragic story "The Death of Ivan Ilyich" is a study in the spiritual effects of ideology. Its hero is a figure who is wholly immersed in the concerns and values of his social class and who is trapped, until the final minutes of his life, in the shallows of shared assumptions. In a central episode, Tolstoy describes the care and delight with which Ivan, suddenly prosperous, fits out his dream house, exactly to his own tastes. The narrator comments:

> In reality it was just what is usually seen in the houses of people of moderate means who want to appear rich, and therefore succeed only in resembling others like themselves: there were damasks, dark wood, plants, rugs, and dull and polished bronzes — all the things people of a certain class have in order to resemble other people of that class. His house was so like the others that it would never have been noticed, but to him it all seemed to be quite exceptional.

Tolstoy implies that Ivan has two distinct motivations: a conscious wish to express his individuality and an unconscious wish to "resemble other people" of his class and time. So thoroughly is he controlled by his class and time that the latter wish dominates the former and even seems identical to it. The town house, his greatest apparent triumph, is a symbol of personal defeat. Slipping as he tries to adjust the curtains in one of his refurnished rooms, Ivan sustains the injury that will bring on his death.

One of the subtlest and most influential forms of ideology is our view of history and our opinion of our own position in it. In this temporal ideology lie not only crucial assumptions about the shape of time but also major elements of our self-image, both as individuals and as a culture. To accept these assumptions and elements without scrutiny is to invest, for better or worse, in the projects or concerns of a single age. It is also to identify with a system whose myth and reality alike are advertised as reality. Time-bound, we can never achieve the historical perspective that is necessary for self-knowledge. Caught between the limited and arbitrary alternatives of a single culture, we cannot develop the moral creativity that allows us to conceive of new alternatives and remake our time.

On the other hand, to challenge our culture's view of history — to ask it directly for its premises and its proofs — is to declare our independence of narrow time and our allegiance to a broader continuum. In so doing we may not only gain new freedom as individuals but also isolate the permanent human aspects of our character from those that come and go with time. Such a study can never be fully successful, since our own present time is at the edge of history, and we cannot examine ourselves in the continuum of past and future. But inquiry into the nature of our own historical assumptions is nonetheless better than nothing. We will be the wiser, to paraphrase Socrates, if only because we know of what we are ignorant.

In this chapter I will try to outline two ways in which we can escape from the tyranny of the present: by viewing the present itself as the making of past time and by using moral philology to examine the verbal bases of our historiographical self-image.

THE PRESENT AS HISTORY

A while ago I experienced, for a few days, a curious sense of living in history. It wasn't the feeling of living at some important time or "charged moment" that was bound to be memorialized in a textbook but the more curious feeling of living, not in the present, but at some indefinite point in the past. Why this feeling should have come, or what were its psychological roots, I could not immediately understand. Instead I decided to enjoy the feeling and to learn from it, as I had not been able to learn before, what the difference is between the way I look at the present and the way I look at the past.

What was suddenly pastlike about my life? When I asked this question, two answers inevitably recurred: that my present life was regular and that it was stylized. By regular I do not mean boring. The daily challenges, in terms of profession and family, were enthralling enough. But the regularity without boredom threw me even deeper into the sense of the past. It struck me that this combination of repetitive order and intense involvement, this narrow avenue of character, was almost a symbol of past time. When we see ourselves in the past, don't we characteristically see people who were consumed, preoccupied? Don't we see people who, limited by their preoccupations, were thus limited by time? Isn't our sense of the past, in part, the sense of people who are enthralled in certain activities and thus diminished by them?

Conversely, our sense of present time is one of width and

openness. The mystique of the present, whether reality or myth, is that we will what we are doing, or at least that what we do not will is endured for the sake of what we do; that we are aware of alternatives and their probable consequences; that we are aware of other viewpoints and their strengths and weaknesses. When our view shifts from past to present and back again, our whole philosophy of life seems to oscillate: we see our past selves as determined, our present selves as free.

But what of the sense of being "stylized"? The word suggests that one's concerns are not merely narrow, but narrow in socially and economically determined ways. What did I do, I asked, that everyone else did? Here the answers were simple. As a middle-class father I was destined, spring and fall, to an indefinite succession of soccer fields, to a sedate fellowship of soccer parents, to the sight of small muddy forms hurtling over grass in fierce play. As the father of young boys I had to fight the good fight, not in theoretical dialogues on freedom and authority, but in terms of specific skateboard trademarks, specific brand names of chemically altered food, specific songs and films made by chemically altered people, specifically unthinkable hair styles and clothing fads. As a suburban homeowner and so-called professional, I had to keep current in memory the variety of reasons why two old V-8 engines might suddenly go dead, the thousand inconveniences of a modern house, the details of departmental squabbles that would vanish in weeks but were potentially catastrophic while they lasted.

What was wrong with these concerns? Nothing, really. What made them feel wrong for me was that I was involved in them automatically, that instead of examining them I was accepting them as finished reality. My acceptance turned me from a potentially independent agent into a kind of puppet. By not challenging and renewing my time I had become caught in it, consigned to the generations who pass as leaves and amalgamate in the humus.

Are we always caught in time this way? One can imagine a clever short story about a hero who was caught in the past, not because he went backward in a time machine and got stuck, but because he could always see an hour or so forward into the clockwork of life. His sense of a programmed future would force in his mind a fusion of past with present.

But his fate need not be our own. Like some homeopathic cure, our very sense of imprisonment can be a step toward liberation. We need not rebel against our temporally determined roles. Merely to recognize them is to limit their power over us. The liberation implied by such awareness is threefold. To understand one's own temporal determinism is to establish, above and beyond what one says and does, an analytic posture toward the present as history; it is to achieve, amid the earnest vanities of contemporary society, an easing humility; it is to mark off, as territory precious and imperiled, the moments and pursuits that are left to our choice.

Such an awareness can also enlighten the sense of the past. The past is perhaps most accurately seen as a continuous present — a carpet feeding seamlessly into the current instant, woven of doing and dreaming, assent and refusal, choice and compulsion. We were as free in the past as we are now, and as enslaved.

This vision of the past would be easier for all of us if great authors habitually took time to describe their own daily lives. Yet such accounts (except in private letters) are remarkably rare in literature. Alone among major writers, Michel de Montaigne excelled at them, describing his own condition in such excellent detail that he is personally more real to us than are most living authors. Here, for example, he speaks of his activities in his library.

> I am over the entrance [to the château], and see below me my garden, my farmyard, my courtyard, and into most of the parts

of my house. There I leaf through now one book, now another, without order and without plan, by disconnected fragments. One moment I muse, another moment I set down or dictate, walking back and forth, these fancies of mine that you see here.

It is on the third floor of a tower; the first is my chapel, the second a bedroom and a dressing room, where I often sleep in order to be alone . . .

The shape of my library is round, the only flat side being the part needed for my table and chair; and curving round me it presents at a glance all my books, arranged in five rows of shelves on all sides. It offers rich and free views in three directions, and sixteen paces of free space in diameter. . . .

There is my throne. I try to make my authority over it absolute, and to withdraw this one corner from all society, conjugal, filial, and civil.

Were other writers too humble to advertise their private compartments in space and time? It is more likely that they were at once too busy and too cautious. Writing about one's own time-locked self won't sell books to present readers, and only affluent amateurs like Montaigne can afford to risk it (ironically, Montaigne sold lots of books). Writing about one's time-locked self risks dangerous personal revelations, unintentional glimpses of the naked self. Montaigne understood the latter danger and indeed courted it. His bold initiative was to describe himself, insofar as possible, "completely naked" (see his preface, "To the Reader"). His greatness lies in his having integrated personal revelation and detail, together with a variety of more conventional humanistic and philosophical methods, in a unique project of self-knowledge and self-liberation.

If good writers were to attempt the specific portraiture of current history, what might such a portrait of time include? First there are the details that make up the immediate substance of daily life and that, just because they do so, are always taken for granted: the schedule of one's day of work or day of leisure, the menu of a breakfast or dinner at home or at a restaurant, the type of transportation one uses and the feelings that it inspires, the nature and effect of household and business machines, the furnishing and decoration of a room. There are the clothing styles and the hair styles and the types of domestic architecture on one's block. There are the social annals: the contents of a news show, the issues debated on the local editorial page, the town projects, the symbols of success, the subjects too loaded to bring up with neighbors, the jokes privately told, the types of clothing that make the sexes attractive to each other, the figurative words used when one wants to make an especially important point, one's ways of expressing anger or other upset, one's most embarrassing memories, the accomplishments in which one takes pride.

Such details, like similar details in the life of one who lived in the 1890s or the reign of Tiberius, may seem uninteresting as subjects for literature, but paradoxically they are uninteresting precisely because they are so obvious. To the future, even a future as near as our children's accession to our own stage of life, they will have the strangeness of an old photograph, and people will wonder how it all must have felt.

LANGUAGE AS HISTORY: THE WORD "MODERN"

Just as we can understand our position in time by projecting ourselves into a context in which we can see ourselves as past, we can understand it by examining key historiographical words and their attendant assumptions. Among such words is one that may be the most ideologically loaded designator in our whole vocabulary. The word is "modern," and it contains a myth.

"Modern" carries with it such vast implications about time

and character that it operates in our communal identity as a kind of hidden middle name. In agreeing that we are modern, we have become perhaps the only age that has ever, self-consciously and unanimously, defined itself against the face of history. We have separated ourselves from the past with barriers which, though assailed by some historians, hold fast in the common mind. We have assumed an identity that we accept as unique and that preserves us, as though behind a wall of glass, from evaluation in terms of traditional models. For us modernity is more than a card of identity or a badge of membership; it is a diplomatic immunity in time, guarding us at once from the judgment of our ancestors and the derision of our offspring.

Indeed, modernity would seem to confer immunity to time itself. Unlike other period words (Victorian, for example, was first used well within Victoria's lifetime), modern does not suggest existence within a definite and limited period. Modern means up-to-date, and up-to-dateness, as all know, is immunity to limit — a ride, as it were, on the crest of the wave.

But what can up-to-dateness mean? Haven't people, no matter when, always conceived of themselves as being up to date? Modernity, however, need not be understood in this silly sense. It implies something much more profound. It implies a radical reorganization of time whose chief premise is that the present is no longer transitory. According to this view, the twentieth century, by virtue of its galloping scientific and technological development, has invaded time itself and usurped the role of historical change. To be modern, in effect, is to move with the speed of time, and to attain this speed is to make time stand still. Modern time can be succeeded by nothing but more modern time. Thus the word "modern" not only suggests the prior existence of periodicity but the earthshaking news that periodicity has come to an end.

Of course few of us, if confronted with it face to face, would wholly endorse the idea of a transfigured history. Although influential voices (advertisements for technology, popular books on science) imply that humanity has conquered time and that we all had better get on the bus, we hold back. It is difficult, perhaps unseemly, to entrust one's full humanity to a system based on chemicals, machines, and circuits. Perhaps for this reason no period has, more than ours, felt the need for physical fitness or the nostalgia for a simpler, more natural life. Are alienation and anxiety the price we must pay for conquering history? Though part of us aspires to it, part of us fears the power that, by allowing us unlimited potentiality for change, might divorce us from our own natures. We fear that in conquering time we may also diminish ourselves.

Another difficulty with the idea of the modern is equally revealing. How do we feel about modernity when one of its paramount symbols — the Chrysler Building or the automat or the Linotype machine — suddenly becomes an antique? That is no problem, replies the modernist, for modernity, as incorporation into change itself, can have no fixed symbols. This inescapable answer leads to a further revelation. If incorporation into change denies fixed symbols, must it not also deny stable values? If one believes in stable moral values, one cannot believe in comprehensive change. One definitely cannot be "up to date" in a society whose primary values flow coherently out of the past. True modernists must be able to shrug off given sets of moral values as carelessly as they shrug off LP records, Edsels, and moon launches.

Unless they are totally nihilistic, ideologies that deny symbols and values have to be based on the material world. The ideology of modernism is no exception to this rule. Material influences, interacting over time, are seen to produce the change that demolishes symbols and alters moral values. The founding doctrines of modernity — Machiavellian, Hobbesian, Newtonian, Marxist, Darwinist, and so forth — stipulate, somehow or other, that all questions can be resolved by reduction to material phenomena. Our two great Western political camps — conservatives who believe in free markets and corporate power, liberals who believe in government controls and equalized wealth — would seem to agree profoundly that the art of government is an art of applied economics. Modernity at large awakes and dreams in awe of a trinity that carries the full charisma of materiality: energy, power, money. Itself impervious to assault, this trinity forges idols and smashes them. Its inner dialectic breeds, on the world's surface, an endless variety of successive forms.

Again, we may not like these implications. We may argue that, though modern, we retain stable values, or we are seeking them; we may deny any sharp break between our time and times past. The implications, nonetheless, remain and are evoked, at least in part, every time the word "modern" is heard, read, or thought. They can be silenced only if we disavow the word "modern" and reawaken to history.

Such a reawakening would require at least two forms of study. First, we should reexamine the origins of the concept of modernity. What idea of historical identity, if any, did "modernity" replace? What other self-identifying terms were its siblings and competitors? In what ways was the denial of periodicity itself a historical artifact?

Second, we should study ways in which "modern" and all other periodic terms, no matter how apt, fall short as comprehensive designators. We may ask how such specific designators measure up against the human characteristics that do not change in time. Appreciating continuity is one of the few legitimate ways of transcending ideology. To appreciate continuity is to stand watching a soccer match and take comfort in the thought that ball games, first described in the West by Homer, are not likely to go out of style. It is to reflect, during some disagreement with one's child, that what is happening has, in essence, always happened between parent and child. It is to find, in some fad or gimmick purporting to be fiendishly up to date, ancient vanity or unintended pathos. Such thoughts will not free us from time, but they are likely to make our imprisonment less debased.

"Modern" of course, is not the only word that describes our historical condition. Our whole current language of interpretation, particularly in speech and writing related to learning, politics, and history, is a historical artifact, a skeleton from which future generations will try to reconstruct the creature that was our time. This language holds keys to our own concerns and limitations. Studying it is like hanging, in a house whose walls have held nothing but flattering portraits, an occasional mirror.

A NOTE ON POSTMODERNISM

In this spirit I should conclude with a note on an effort to define modernity as time past. The term "postmodernism" is currently used either by artists and thinkers wishing to distinguish their own productions from those of the recent past, or by historical theorists wishing to characterize certain contemporary trends as a generic departure from modernity. "Postmodernism," as now employed, is a convenient catchall for enterprises as diverse as neoclassicism, neo-Victorianism and other forms of architectural nostalgia, and poststructuralist vogues like deconstruction. In other words, anything from traditionalism to futurism, anything from absolutism to anarchy, can be labeled postmodern.

Herein lies part of my dislike for the term. In the manner of "one size fits all," postmodernism is used to encompass everything, and consequently describes nothing. There simply is not enough coherence in the things described as postmodern to show that they partake of a common spirit, to prove that the sands in our glass have at last run out and that we are entering new times. Suddenly proclaiming ourselves to be postmodern or anything else bespeaks ideological vanity. Why not just do our best and leave it to future historians to decide what we were and when?

Postmodernism, moreover, is an ugly term — ugly, ironically, in a very modern way. To describe anything as merely being "post" something else is to deprive it of character, and nothing is more characteristic of modern thought than its habit of depriving itself and everything else of character. Bitterer irony lies in the fact that postmodernism, formally considered, is a contradiction in terms: how can anything be post-up-to-date? If modernism is (as I hope) going to be followed by something, and soon, and if that something has to have a name to know itself by, that name ought to have more substance and coherence than postmodernism.

23 Conclusion

IN 1979 the English biologist J. E. Lovelock brought forth in print a startling idea. The earth, he wrote, was (with its atmosphere) a living thing, an organically interrelated system with global mechanisms of governance and response. Named Gaia by William Golding, Lovelock's theory has prompted many scientists and laymen to reconsider their assumptions about the earth and life.

The strength of the Gaia hypothesis (which actually depends on how we define the phrase "living thing") is not at issue here. What interests me is that a theory quite like Lovelock's was advanced in ancient Greece and enjoyed literate popularity for several centuries. It was mooted in Plato's *Timaeus*, which I referred to in Chapter 6. Lovelock apparently was unaware of the link with the *Timaeus* when he published his theory, which was received by supporters and critics alike as something entirely new.

Ernst Cassirer drew attention to another key link between modern innovation and ancient theory when he showed that Galileo was consciously indebted to Plato and Archimedes in his "innovative" use of the hypothetical method. A third and more general continuity between ancient and modern received special emphasis from Michael Polanyi, who wrote of modern physics:

The beauty and power inherent in the rationality of contemporary physics is, as I have said, of a novel kind. When classical physics superseded the Pythagorean tradition, mathematical theory was reduced to a mere instrument for computing the mechanical motions which were supposed to underlie all natural phenomena. Geometry also stood outside nature, claiming to offer an a priori analysis of Euclidean space, which was regarded as the scene of all natural phenomena but not thought to be involved in them. Relativity, and subsequently quantum mechanics and modern physics generally, have moved back towards a mathematical conception of reality . . . [Thus] modern physics has demonstrated the power of the human mind to discover and exhibit a rationality which governs nature . . . Thus relativity has restored, up to a point, the blend of geometry and physics which Pythagorean thought had first naively taken for granted.

By implication, Polanyi credits modern physics with establishing three major forms of continuity: the integral relationship between abstract idea (calculus, geometry) and natural phenomena; the more general continuity between human reason and "a rationality which governs nature"; and the consistency of modern innovation with ancient (Pythagorean and also Platonic) philosophy. To Polanyi, Einstein's quasi-Pythagorean insight is more than a coincidence or a meeting of minds. Instead it is, simply put, the restoration of the proper relation between science and the cosmos, between mind and nature. Polanyi uses the relativity example to support his major thesis that there are permanent communalities between the principles on which we base our vision of nature and the principles behind the nature we see.

Does the fact that the Lovelock hypothesis had an ancient precursor make Lovelock less original? Were Galileo and Einstein less innovative for having been anticipated by pagan antiquity? By modern standards, which equate discovery with the "completely different," "unprecedented," and "unique," the answer to both questions would have to be yes. But the examples just described suggest that such standards should be applied with caution.

We should remember, first of all, that Lovelock, Galileo, and Einstein developed their ideas in historical contexts entirely different from those inhabited by Pythagoras and Plato, and they applied these ideas in ways that had not previously been imagined. We must note as well that human history, as expressed in such things as style, language, and technology, is subject to endless permutations. It follows that the innovative power of ideas should be measured not by only their comparative uniqueness but also by their impact on a given historical context. Because historical contexts change radically, the same idea, applied from period to period, can be authentically innovative, and much material for valid innovation resides in the treasury of things past. The inexorable operation of change paradoxically bestows newness on the past.

This paradox suggests another. Both natural science and humanistic inquiry are quests for general law, and it is a prerequisite of general law to apply not only comprehensively but permanently. Discovery is therefore "transforming" or "innovative" in direct proportion to the permanence of what is discovered. It is tempting to say that innovation is the art of discovering what is old. More diplomatically put, it is the art of drawing oneself into conversance with what is permanent. Innovative vision and creative achievement of all sorts are based on the imperturbable regularity of things.

Thus creativity and innovation, for all their vaunted liberties, are deeply tied to continuities human and natural. We cannot innovate in science without enlarging our appreciation for timeless laws. We cannot innovate in art or philosophy without renewing contact with ancient issues. I have compared innovative thinking to a voyage, and its territory to a frontier. But paradoxically it is also a homecoming, a heroic effort, by individuals exiled in space and time, to realize principles of solidarity and permanence.

Because of the mysterious doubleness of creative identity, neither the typical liberal attitude nor the typical conservative attitude toward innovation is wholly constructive. Modern liberalism endorses innovation as the medium of radically transfiguring improvement. Modern conservatism distrusts innovation, instead supporting stability (preservation of the status quo) or rededication (return to values putatively held in the past). Liberalism and conservatism would offer us valid alternatives — and even prove happy complements to each other — if innovative discovery were purely and simply the discovery of the new.

But this is not the case. If the real subject of discovery is not novelty but permanence, then real innovation lies not in the denial of permanence but in the evolution of our modes of perceiving it. Ill at ease with continuity of any sort, modern liberalism is insensitive to many forms of valid innovation. Modern conservatism, on the other hand, misinterprets as monolithic stability a continuity that can be retained only through evolving methods.

Innovation is thus neither liberal nor conservative. At heart it is decidedly more primitive. It belongs to the poet and the hero.

Notes

PAGE

xiii Rilke, *Rodin,* trans. Robert Firmage (Salt Lake City: Peregrine Smith, 1979).

Chapter 1. Introduction

PAGE

3-4 The two famous books I refer to are, nonetheless, among my favorites: Bernard J. F. Lonergan, *Insight* (New York: Longman, 1958; Harper & Row, 1978), and Michael Polanyi, *Personal Knowledge* (London: Routledge and Kegan Paul, 1958; Chicago: University of Chicago Press, 1962). For the psychological approach to creativity, the best introduction is Albert Rothenberg and Carl R. Hausman's collection of excerpts, *The Creativity Question* (Durham: Duke University Press, 1976).

8 Bach was widely regarded, in his own time, as a competent but uninspired traditionalist. He lived to see his Baroque style upstaged by early Classicism and his fame eclipsed by that of his sons, Karl Philipp Emanuel and Johann Christian. Mozart received a pauper's funeral and was buried in an unmarked grave. Van Gogh lived and died in obscurity. Other artists who endured public neglect were Keats, Bizet, and Melville. The list of Nobel Prize laureates in literature includes many forgotten names but notably excludes Joseph Conrad and Henry James.

Chapter 2. Inspiration

10   Lonergan, *Insight*, 3; Kepler is quoted by R. W. Gerard in *The Creative Process,* ed. Brewster Ghiselin (Berkeley: University of California Press, 1952, 1985), 259.

12–13   On the work/leisure distinction see my essay, "The Humanity of Leisure," in B. J. Gunter, Jay Stanley, and Robert St. Clair, eds., *Transitions to Leisure* (Lanham, Md./New York/London: University Press of America, 1985), 113–118.

17–18   Innocence and Playfulness: Ernest G. Schachtel describes similar "childlike" characteristics in analyses of the creative process. Schachtel emphasizes the role of "free and open play of attention" in creativity. Such attention, he writes, "may at times be playful, too; but that is not its main characteristic. It resembles the child's free play in his encounter with the world where playfulness, too, is not the main factor but the openness, the intensity of the interest, the repeated and varied approaches, which range all the way from the grave and serious, to the playful and fleeting" *(Metamorphosis: On the Development of Affect, Perception, Attention and Memory* [New York: Basic Books, 1959], 241f.) For Carl R. Rogers, creativity owes in part to "the ability to play spontaneously with ideas, colors, shapes, relationships — to juggle elements into impossible juxtapositions, to express the ridiculous, to translate from one form into another, to transform into improbable equivalents. It is from this spontaneous toying and exploration that there arises the hunch, the creative seeing of life in a new and significant way" ("Toward a Theory of Creativity," *ETC: A Review of General Semantics* 11, 4, [1954]: 255). Both passages are quoted by Rothenberg and Hausman in *The Creativity Question,* 157, 301.

19   Suffering: In *The Courage to Create* (New York: Norton, 1975; Bantam, 1976) Rollo May describes two experiences (one from his own professional career and one from the life of the scientist Henri Poincaré) in which inspiration broke upon individual researchers who had apparently exhausted all rational means of solving problems at hand. Paraphrasing Poincaré, he characterizes the experience of inspiration as follows: "(1) the suddenness of the illumination; (2) the fact that the insight may occur, and to some extent must occur, as a contradiction to what one has clung to consciously in one's theories; (3) the vividness of the incident and the whole scene that surrounds it; (4) the brevity and conciseness of the insight, along with the experience of immediate certainty . . . ; (5) hard work on the topic prior to the breakthrough; (6) a rest, in which the 'unconscious work' has

been given a chance to proceed on its own and after which the break-through may occur," 70f. May's thesis is that inspiration comes from sources in the unconscious that are stimulated by conscious "hard work" and then liberated by the "rest" that follows it. I find this model accurate as far as it goes, but think that it ignores one factor: the pure pain — annoyance, anger, frustration, humiliation, whatever — that accompanies the failure of conscious or rational solutions and makes the mind fertile for inspiration. And here is the irony of inspiration: that these agonies, which in the lives of creative people promise and prefigure inspirations to come, are exactly what cause the rest of us to abandon work in progress.

20–21   A Sense of the Continuity of Perception: See Arthur Koestler, *The Act of Creation* (New York: Macmillan, 1964).

Chapter 3. Discovery

PAGE

24   Remark attributed to Charles Darwin by his wife, Emma. *The Autobiography of Charles Darwin* (1887; New York: Dover, 1969), 159.

28ff.   For Thomas Kuhn's theory of anomaly see *The Structure of Scientific Revolutions* (Chicago: University of Chicago Press, 1962; 2d enlarged ed., 1970), Chap. 6.

30   For Peter Drucker's theory of anomaly see *Innovation and Entrepreneurship* (New York: Harper & Row, 1985), I.4.

Chapter 4. Analysis

PAGE

34   Wright: *Autobiography* (New York: Longman's, Green, 1932), 148; Whitehead: "The Education of an Englishman," *Atlantic*, 138 (1926): 197.

44   Polanyi's comment is from *Personal Knowledge*, 143. For Maurois's remark on youthfulness, see *Disraeli*, English ed., trans. Hamish Miles (New York: D. Appleton, 1928), final sentence.

N.B. For my treatment of Task, Problem, and Mystery in this chapter I am indebted to conversations with Svi Lanir, whose concept of "fundamental surprise" held the germ of the concept I call Mystery.

In an earlier draft I cited different examples of Task, Problem, and Mystery. Because they may be useful as an additional point of reference, I include them here.

Challenge Type A, Task: Mr. Finch returns home from two weeks in the mountains to find the interior of his house drenched in water. A gurgling noise from the bathroom makes extensive investigation unnecessary. Finch's plumbing tools are in the garage, and he resorts to them.

Challenge Type B, Problem: Mr. Finch returns from the mountains to find that his house has disappeared from the face of the earth. Where that amiable structure once stood, there remains only a flat, bare patch of earth. No official notice or charred timber or telltale of any kind suggests the cause of disappearance. Before he can take action of any sort, Finch needs more information.

Challenge Type C, Mystery: Mr. Finch returns from the mountains to find his house exactly as he had left it, in perfect shape. He moves in and resumes his usual duties and recreations. But after a week or so he begins to feel unaccountably uncomfortable in his quarters. Has Finch at last become aware of some inadequacy latent in the structure? Has he outgrown his old domestic tastes? Is he merely in a prolonged bad mood? The problem is difficult to define, much less to reduce. It threatens to persist, like a ghostly shadow, unless it is illuminated by insight.

Chapter 5. Imagination

PAGE

46   Castiglione, *The Book of the Courtier* (1528), trans. Charles S. Singleton (Garden City, N.Y.: Doubleday, 1959), II.70.

53f.   Gordon, "On Being Explicit about Creative Process," *Journal of Creative Behavior* 6 (1972): 295–300; quoted in *The Creativity Question,* 251f. "Strangeness," as Gordon describes it in "On Being Explicit," is a property quite similar to "anomaly," as introduced in Chapter 3.

Chapter 6. The Sense of Beauty

PAGE

56   Bateson, *Mind and Nature* (New York: Dutton, 1979), 8. On beauty in science, see, for example, K. C. Cole, *Sympathetic Vibrations* (New York: Morrow, 1984; Bantam, 1985), Chap. 10; and Paul Davies, *Superforce* (London: Heinemann, 1984), 53ff. Also see James Gleick's treatment of the Mandelbrot set in *Chaos* (New York: Viking Penguin, 1987), 81–118, 213–240.

58f. Joyce, *Stephen Hero* (unfinished ms., 1904-1906; first published 1944; London: Ace Books, 1961), 188.

59-60 For Plato's comments on beauty and philosophy, see the *Symposium*, 210a-212c, and the *Phaedrus*, 244a-249d.

62 A zoologist might reasonably disagree with my comments on ugliness, holding that evolution itself is a "free" process in which new life forms continually take shape and (as they meet or fail the test of life) are accepted or rejected by their environment. The word "beauty" could then be applied to those forms which thrive, since they have wholeness both in themselves and in terms of their relationship to the environment. "Ugliness" could be applied to those forms which are rejected or, having been successful, are rendered obsolete by environmental change.

64ff. Viktor Frankl, *Man's Search for Meaning* (Boston: Beacon Press, 1959; New York: Washington Square Press, 1985), 90.

Chapter 7. Introduction

PAGE

70 Whitehead's comment is from *The Aims of Education* (New York: Macmillan, 1929), 19.

Chapter 8. Integrity

PAGE

72 Frost, "Mowing," *Collected Poems* (New York: Holt, Rinehart and Winston, 1964), 25.

75f. The Maslow passage is from *Toward a Psychology of Being* (New York: Van Nostrand Reinhold, 1968), 135-141, 143, 145, and is quoted in *The Creativity Question*, 89.

76f. The Darwin anecdote is from *The Autobiography of Charles Darwin*, 62.

Donald's account of Thomas Wolfe's present is from *The New York Times Review of Books*, January 11, 1987, 35.

85 On wise deceit in the Renaissance, see, for example, Francis Bacon's essay "Of Truth" or Shakespeare's *Measure for Measure* or *King Lear*, in which major characters (the Duke and Edgar, respectively), distressed or endangered by events in the world around them, spend much of their time in disguise.

Chapter 9. Pain

PAGE
86   Shakespeare, *King Lear,* IV, vi, 221–223 (spoken by Edgar).

Chapter 10. Courage

PAGE
96   Polanyi, *Personal Knowledge,* viii; Man Ray, quoted by Helen Dudar in her article "The Man Who Invented Himself, and Kept Right on Inventing," *Smithsonian,* December 1988, 67.
       Rollo May, *The Courage to Create* (New York: Norton, 1975; Bantam, 1976), 14f., 26.
109   The classical views on courage may be found in Plato, *Protagoras,* 360d, and Aristotle, *Nicomachean Ethics,* 1115b.

Chapter 11. Self-knowledge

PAGE
110   Plato, *Sophist,* 263e.
111   The dialogue in this chapter is based on the Platonic model but differs from it intentionally in one respect: in Plato, Socrates or some other expert teacher dominates the conversation and, through questioning or narrative, induces or provides all major revelations. In my dialogue Marlin is the expert teacher, but it is the "student" Simmons who is inspired with the major ideas. I wrote it this way to illustrate my contentions that inspiration is born of pain and frustration and that the true teacher can induce creativity in the student through surprise and challenge.

Chapter 12. Freedom

PAGE
127   Montesquieu, *The Spirit of the Laws,* XI. 3; Plato, Eighth Letter, 354e.
128   Bergson's *Time and Free Will* appeared in 1889; Croce's *History as the Story of Liberty* in 1938. Mill's *On Liberty* dates from 1859.

Solzhenitsyn's Commencement Address, delivered at Harvard University on June 8, 1978, has been reprinted as *A World Split Apart* (New York: Harper & Row, 1978). Note especially the sections entitled Legalistic Life (15–19) and The Direction of Freedom (19–23).

132f.   Peter F. Drucker, *Innovation and Entrepreneurship* (New York: Harper & Row, 1985), 62f.

135   In quoting Saint Paul, I have used the New English Bible (n.p.), Cambridge University Press and Oxford University Press, 1970. Later biblical quotations are from the King James Version.

Chapter 13. Introduction

PAGE

139   Details about Beethoven's Great Fugue were drawn from Martin Cooper, *Beethoven: The Last Decade* (London: Oxford University Press, 1970), 381. Drebbel's English biographer is L. E. Harris *(The Two Netherlanders: Humphrey Bradley and Cornelis Drebbel* [Cambridge, England: Heffer, 1961]).

142   Lonergan's comment on "automatic Progress" is in *Insight,* 240f.

Chapter 14. On Teaching

PAGE

146   Plato, *Theaetetus,* 155d.

149f.   Fritz (Arthur Anderson) Peters, *Boyhood with Gurdjieff* (London: Gollancz, 1964), Chap. 1–4. For Plato's views on teaching and self-knowledge see, for example, the *Timaeus,* 47b–c: "God invented and gave us sight to the end that we might behold the courses of intelligence in the heaven, and apply them to the courses of our own intelligence that are akin to them, the unperturbed to the perturbed. And that we, learning them and partaking of the general truth of reason, might imitate the absolutely unerring courses of God and regulate our own vagaries." Benjamin Jowett, trans., *The Collected Dialogues of Plato, ed. Edith Hamilton and Huntington Cairns* (Princeton: Princeton University Press, 1963), 1175. Also see the *Timaeus,* 90d–e.

152f.   Cellini's tale of his childhood is from *The Autobiography of Benvenuto Cellini* (composed 1558–1562; published 1730), trans. Robert Hobart Cust (New York: Dodd, Mead, 1961), 9f.

153   Gurdjieff recounts his adventure with the dervish in *Meetings with Remarkable Men* (New York: Dutton, 1969, 1974), 186.

Chapter 15. Higher Education and Classical Wholeness

PAGE

155 Montaigne, *Essays,* trans. Donald Frame (Stanford: Stanford University Press, 1965), 117.

157 Plato's criticism of specialists occurs in the *Apology,* 21c–22e; his views on dialectic, synopsis, and interdisciplinary education are to be found in the *Republic,* Book 7, and the *Symposium,* 210b–211e.

163f. Aristotle's endorsement of interdisciplinary education is implied in his statement that politics, as the "master science," contains other important sciences. *Nicomachean Ethics,* 1094a–b.

Chapter 16. Vision, Learning, and Power

PAGE

165 Ortega y Gasset, *The Revolt of the Masses,* trans. anon. (New York: Norton, 1957), 114.

Chapter 17. Philosophy and the Equation of Being

PAGE

175 "The Woman in Sunshine" (see also p. 179) is from *The Collected Poems of Wallace Stevens* (New York: Knopf, 1955), 445; Marvell's "The Garden" is widely anthologized.

180 Plato, *Timaeus,* 29a–34b; *Phaedrus,* 264c.

183 See, for example, Bateson, *Mind and Nature;* Edward O. Wilson, *Biophilia* (Cambridge, Mass.: Harvard University Press, 1984); Lewis Thomas, *Late Night Thoughts on Listening to Mahler's Ninth Symphony* (New York: Viking, 1983); Ilya Prigogine and Isabelle Stengers, *Order Out of Chaos* (New York: Bantam, 1984); Stephen Jay Gould, "Triumph of a Naturalist," *New York Review of Books* 31, 5, (March 29, 1984): 3–6; Polanyi, *Personal Knowledge.*

Chapter 18. Art

PAGE

185 Joseph Conrad, *The Nigger of the "Narcissus"* (1897), Preface.

189 Aristotle introduces the idea of catharsis in the *Poetics,* Chap. 6. For the idea of mimesis, see Chap. 1–6, passim; and Plato, *Republic* (Book 3), 393c–398c.

Chapter 19. The Diplomacy of Invention

PAGE

197   Machiavelli, *The Prince* (1532), Chap. 6 (my translation).

199f.   The story is from Castiglione, *The Book of the Courtier*, II. 51.

202f.   On Drebbel's solar heating plan, see Harris, *The Two Netherlanders,* 189-191. On his demonstration of refrigeration, see Richard Brenchley Rye, *England as Seen by Foreigners in the Days of Elizabeth and James I* (1865; New York: Benjamin Blom, 1967), 234.

205-   The Shakespeare passage (Sonnet 110, lines 1-8) runs as follows:
206

> Alas, 'tis true, I have gone here and there,
> And made myself a motley to the view,
> Gor'd mine own thoughts, sold cheap what is most dear,
> Made old offenses of affections new;
> Most true it is that I have look'd on truth
> Askance and strangely: but by all above,
> These blenches gave my heart another youth,
> And worse essays prov'd thee my best of love.

Chapter 20. The Eyes of Laughter

PAGE

208   Marx's comment is reported in Dorothy Herrman, *S. J. Perelman: A Life* (New York: G. P. Putnam's Sons, 1986), 61.

208ff.   The theory of laughter presented here is both an outgrowth and a departure from tradition. Cicero held influentially that the subject of laughter was "deformity" (*De oratore,* 2; also see Castiglione, *The Book of the Courtier,* Book 2, 45-46). Modern theory of laughter is indebted to Henri Bergson's *Le Rire* (1900; published in English as *Laughter* [London: Macmillan, 1911]); Bergson maintains that the "funny" is "mechanical" action on the part of human subjects. My theory of laughter takes Bergson's, reverses it from a critique of the mechanical to a critique of the "free," and combines it with Aristotle's theory of tragic catharsis.

Chapter 21. Ideology and Moral Philology

PAGE

218   Bacon, *Novum Organum* (1620), I.59; Mark Twain, *Pudd'nhead Wilson* (1893-1894; New York: Bantam, 1959), Chap. 15.

Chapter 22. The Ideology of Present Time

PAGE
228 Pascal, *Pensées* (1670), IV.1; Tolstoy, "The Death of Ivan Ilyich" (1886), trans. Louise and Aylmer Maude, in the *Norton Anthology of World Masterpieces,* 5th ed. (New York: Norton, 1985), 1194.

232– Montaigne, *Essays,* III.3.
233

Chapter 23. Conclusion

PAGE
240f. Lovelock, *Gaia: A New Look at Life on Earth* (Oxford and New York: Oxford University Press, 1979); Polanyi, *Personal Knowledge,* 14f.; Cassirer, "Galileo's Platonism," in *Studies and Essays in the History of Science and Learning,* ed. M. F. Ashley Montagu (New York: Schuman, 1946), 277–297.

Works Cited

Aristotle. *Nicomachean Ethics, Poetics.*

Bateson, Gregory, *Mind and Nature.* New York: Dutton, 1979.

Bergson, Henri. *Laughter.* London: Macmillan, 1911.

Cassirer, Ernst. "Galileo's Platonism," in *Studies and Essays in the History of Science and Learning,* ed. M. F. Ashley Montagu. New York: Schuman, 1946.

Castiglione, Baldassare. *The Book of the Courtier,* trans. Charles S. Singleton. Garden City, N.Y.: Doubleday Anchor, 1959.

Cellini, Benvenuto. *The Autobiography of Benvenuto Cellini,* trans. Robert Hobart Cust. New York: Dodd, Mead, 1961.

Cole, K. C. *Sympathetic Vibrations.* New York: Morrow, 1984; Bantam, 1985.

Conrad, Joseph. *The Nigger of the "Narcissus,"* 1897.

Cooper, Martin. *Beethoven: The Last Decade.* London: Oxford University Press, 1970.

Darwin, Charles. *The Autobiography of Charles Darwin.* New York: Dover, 1969.

Davies, Paul. *Superforce.* London: Heinemann, 1984.

Donald, David Herbert. "Wolfe in Love." *The New York Times Review of Books,* January 11, 1987.

Drucker, Peter F. *Innovation and Entrepreneurship.* New York: Harper & Row, 1985.

Dudar, Helen. "The Man Who Invented Himself, and Kept Right on Inventing." *Smithsonian,* December 1988.

Frankl, Viktor. *Man's Search for Meaning.* New York: Washington Square Press, 1985.

Frost, Robert. *Collected Poems.* New York: Holt, Rinehart and Winston, 1964.

Ghiselin, Brewster, ed. *The Creative Process*. Berkeley: University of California Press, 1952, 1985.

Gleick, James. *Chaos*. New York: Viking Penguin, 1987.

Gordon, William J. J. "On Being Explicit about Creative Process." *Journal of Creative Behavior 6* (1972).

Gould, Stephen Jay. "Triumph of a Naturalist." *New York Review of Books* 31, 5 (March 29, 1984).

Grudin, Robert. "The Humanity of Leisure," in B. J. Gunter, Jay Stanley, and Robert St. Clair, eds., *Transitions to Leisure*. Lanham, Md./New York/London: University Press of America, 1985.

Gurdjieff, G. I. *Meetings with Remarkable Men*. New York: Dutton, 1969, 1974.

Harris, L. E. *The Two Netherlanders: Humphrey Bradley and Cornelis Drebbel*. Cambridge, England: Heffer, 1961.

Herrman, Dorothy. *S. J. Perelman: A Life*. New York: G. P. Putnam's Sons, 1986.

Joyce, James. *Stephen Hero*. London: Ace Books, 1961.

Koestler, Arthur. *The Act of Creation*. New York: Macmillan, 1964.

Kuhn, Thomas. *The Structure of Scientific Revolutions*. Chicago: University of Chicago Press, 1962; 2d enlarged ed. 1970.

Lonergan, Bernard J. F. *Insight*. 1958; New York: Harper & Row, 1978.

Lovelock, James. *Gaia: A New Look at Life on Earth*. Oxford and New York: Oxford University Press, 1979.

Maslow, Abraham. *Toward a Psychology of Being*. New York: Van Nostrand Reinhold, 1968.

Maurois, André. *Disraeli*, trans. Hamish Miles. New York: D. Appleton, 1928.

May, Rollo. *The Courage to Create*. New York: Bantam, 1976.

Ortega y Gasset, José. *The Revolt of the Masses*, trans. anon. New York: Norton, 1957.

Peters, Fritz (Arthur Anderson). *Boyhood with Gurdjieff*. London: Gollancz, 1964.

Plato. *Protagoras, Sophist, Eighth Letter, Theaetetus, Timaeus, Republic, Symposium*.

Polanyi, Michael. *Personal Knowledge*. 1958; Chicago: University of Chicago Press, 1962.

Prigogine, Ilya, and Stengers, Isabelle. *Order Out of Chaos*. New York: Bantam, 1984.

Rilke, Rainer Maria. *Rodin*, trans. Robert Firmage. Salt Lake City: Peregrine Smith, 1979.

Rogers, Carl. "Toward a Theory of Creativity," in *ETC: A Review of General Semantics* 11, 4 (1954).

Rothenberg, Albert, and Hausman, Carl R. *The Creativity Question*. Durham: Duke University Press, 1976.

Rye, Richard Brenchley. *England as Seen by Foreigners in the Days of Elizabeth and James I*. New York: Benjamin Blom, 1967.

Schachtel, Ernest G. *Metamorphosis: On the Development of Affect, Perception, Attention and Memory* (New York: Basic Books, 1959), 241f.

Solzhenitsyn, Aleksandr. *A World Split Apart*. New York: Harper & Row, 1978.

Stevens, Wallace, *Collected Poems*. New York: Knopf, 1955.

Thomas, Lewis. *Late Night Thoughts on Listening to Mahler's Ninth Symphony*. New York: Viking, 1983.

Tolstoy, Leo. "The Death of Ivan Ilyich," trans. Louis and Aylmer Maude, in the *Norton Anthology of World Masterpieces*, 5th ed. New York: Norton, 1985.

Twain, Mark. *Pudd'nhead Wilson*. New York: Bantam, 1959.

Whitehead, Alfred North. *The Aims of Education*. New York: Macmillan, 1929.

——. "The Education of an Englishman." *Atlantic*, 138 (1926).

Wilson, Edward O. *Biophilia*. Cambridge, Mass.: Harvard University Press, 1984.

Wright, Frank Lloyd. *Autobiography*. New York: Longman's, Green, 1932.